In Search of the
New America

Lee Somerstein

Copyright © 2013 Lee Somerstein

All rights reserved.

ISBN-13: 978-1494334499
ISBN-10: 1494334496

In Search of the New America

This book is dedicated to Jim (Stutz Bearcat) Stutzman whose friendship and support for this project are invaluable.

Preface

Home, Home on the Road

This book is about a road trip. It's not just another "On the Road" book because this was not just any road trip. I was seeking answers and I needed to talk to Americans across the country to find them.

While the Great Recession is in many of our rear view mirrors, its affects are not. The recovery for many is slow and, as I suspected when I started my trip, non-existent for others. What I do know is the recession changed America and Americans. It changed the way governments govern (and pay to deliver their services), the way businesses large and small conduct their business and, most importantly, it changed the way families finance their lives. This trip was about chronicling these changes through the stories of people across the socio-economic spectrum of this great land.

The idea for the book germinated as I experienced my own dramatic changes and mine is the first story to tell. The Great Recession altered my life forever and in ways I never imagined possible.

Throughout my career, first as a broadcast journalist and again as a marketing/public relations professional, I experienced varying levels of success. The one constant, however, was that I continually maintained a comfortable lifestyle; I could always pay my bills while also enjoying a few simple luxuries – and one BIG one.

Following my 2005 divorce, and subsequent sale of our house, I fulfilled a lifelong dream and made the most extravagant purchase of my life, a used, cherry condition 2003 Porsche Boxster S. It was midnight blue with a lighter blue convertible top and saddle tan leather throughout. The 256 HP engine, mounted behind and below the two seats howled at the top end like a jet engine. With the mid-engine configuration, the Boxster S is one of the best handling cars in the world. It sparkled on the road and in my heart.

My Dear Departed Porsche Boxster S

Honestly, I am not an extravagant man. I never went in for all the "toys" that go with middle-class success. The Porsche was the one exception; I'd wanted one forever and I've never regretted it.

In January 2007 I made a series of decisions aimed at improving an already good life. I left a long-standing, comfortable position for a new challenge. Safeco Insurance, a Fortune 500 company and Washington State's largest insurance carrier, hired me as their Media Relations Manager. Not only was it my first high-level job with a major corporation – I'd worked mostly in the public sector – it would also pay me more money than I'd ever earned in my life.

Shortly thereafter I rolled over my retirement account, nearly $250,000, into a down payment on a beautiful townhouse along the Green River, about 20 miles southeast of Seattle. The manager of my retirement fund agreed it was a good move; the fund was earning about nine percent annually while housing prices were still racing ahead at almost 15 percent. Indeed, life was good. Then, it turned bad, very bad.

Like dominos, my good decisions began to fall, each one knocking down the other. A few months after I closed on my townhouse the real estate bubble burst and values began to slide. Not too long after that, The Great Recession became official. In December 2007 a series of record storms swelled rivers throughout the region and the Green River's Howard Hanson Dam began to leak.

The earthen Howard Hanson Dam was built in the mid-20th Century to control catastrophic flooding in the verdant Green River Valley. When it began to leak at the end of 2007 the Army Corps of Engineers warned the threat of catastrophic flooding increased dramatically. My home value no longer slid; it plummeted.

Finally, in January 2008, the last domino fell. Immediately after I started at Safeco in early 2007 I heard rumblings of a possible acquisition by a national insurance company. Almost one year to the day after I was hired, Safeco began eliminating "headquarters positions." Mine was the first job axed. Safeco was eventually taken over by Liberty Mutual.

I know how to job-hunt. I have a very strong resume and I interview well. There was one problem; I was 61 years old. Even as I made it to the final round for several jobs, the term "over qualified" was usually used to explain why I wasn't hired. To me, overqualified sounded like a legal way of saying "too old."

Over the next 18 months I went from sitting with my ass in a tub of butter to selling my Porsche (sob!), watching a pile of unpaid bills take over my desk, losing my health insurance and, finally short selling my townhouse one week before the foreclosure hearing. It sold for $140,000 less than I paid. I was destitute.

I'd never faced poverty in my life and now I was about to be homeless. The good news is I am blessed with amazing people in my life, including one very special woman who took me in and gave me a home.

The best news is I refused to feel defeat or despair. After a fruitless three-year job search I started a small business with limited success but not enough to pull me out of the hole. It was at that point the germ for this book began to blossom. I knew my experience wasn't unique and I began to wonder about The Great Recession's personal toll across America.

So, I hit the road.

Chapter 1 – First Leg: Starting Close to Home

Thursday July 11 – Seattle to Everett and Guemes Island, WA

The City of Everett (pop. 103,000) sits in Seattle's shadow 25 miles to the north. This old mill town is a fitting place to start my journey. Early in its history Everett rode the economic ups and downs of the railroad, mining and timber industries.

In 1916 the city endured one of the early labor movement's most violent confrontations, The Everett Massacre, between members of the Industrial Workers of the World (The Wobblies) and local law enforcement aligned with the business community. It came during a shingles workers strike and an economic depression. Twenty people died with more than 40 wounded in the gunfire.

Today Everett is home for one of Boeing's major airplane construction plants and serves as a U.S. Navy Home Port, both great for the local economy. As a result, the city is ahead of the nation's economic recovery. Its county, Snohomish, has the second lowest unemployment rate in the state at 4.9%. That doesn't mean the Great Recession went down easily here.

My first stop is a Safeway along Highway 99 about seven miles south of downtown Everett. This part of 99 is six lanes peppered by traffic lights and dotted with strip malls, used car lots, casinos, cheap apartments and cheaper motels. Safeway's customers reflect the surroundings.

Standing for about a half hour in the parking lot I talked to a retired Boeing engineer who told me the recession left him mostly untouched. "Maybe inflation hurt a little," he said, "but I kept my head down and Boeing's pension plan is pretty good."

Not true for the woman who is both nameless and homeless. She won't share her name but she does share her story. Before the recession she'd been in her home for fourteen years, supported by her boyfriend's income as a carpenter. As the housing market crashed, the carpentry work dried up until her boyfriend could no longer meet his house payments. Unfortunately, he turned to dealing, then using, methamphetamine to try to make ends meet. You know how that story ends. This 46-year old woman, who looks at least

15-years older, now lives under a bridge and takes in small sewing jobs to buy food. The boyfriend is gone.

Moving north to the Amtrak/commuter rail station and transit center near downtown, I hear from a 25-year old woman who contracts out doing corporate writing for clients. As the recession deepened the jobs became fewer and fewer. "It was tough," she tells me, "but I learned how to persevere and how to handle a crisis. Today I save more of my income than I did before the recession."

Then there's Neil Tilly, a 35-year old roofer waiting for an Amtrak train to take him home to Wenatchee, in eastern Washington. Before the recession he spent four years working construction in Reno. As construction slowed to a standstill he found himself out of work and back home in Wenatchee.

"Instead of working," he says matter-of-factly, "I was sitting in bars and drinking too much. I got into a fight and spent two years in prison – first time I've been trouble. The whole experience changed me, both unemployment and prison. Today, I'm more cautious in life and I don't drink anymore."

Tilly is employed again, doing commercial flat roofs in Wenatchee but, he says, there's not as much work as there was before the crash.

My last interview in Everett is Mayor Ray Stephanson. It's a whole different ball game on the tenth floor of the commercial building that serves as City Hall. Mayor Stephanson emerges from an earlier meeting dressed in a conservative yet natty suit, his blonde hair streaked with grey and neatly coiffed. He could be a TV news anchorman.

We sit in a big conference room with a picture window showcasing one of Everett's greatest assets, a panoramic view of Puget Sound and the mighty Olympic Mountains hovering on the western horizon across the sound on the Olympic Peninsula. I've lived in Seattle for 39-years and the views all around still stagger me.

Stephanson has ten years in office and even before the recession, he says he took measures he calls protective in the face of any economic situation, cutting costs, reducing debt and basically streamlining. Still the recession hit hard.

"Because we were as ready as we could be," he told me, "we did not have to cut first responders' services but we cut in many other small ways to face the crisis and we came through it pretty well compared to other cities."

Post recession, though, things *are* different. "It significantly affected people's spending habits," he says. "Our sales tax revenue hasn't recovered yet; it is down 20% from pre-recession years and I call that the 'new norm.'"

In 2012 the mayor earned $154,956.72. I have no idea how the city council arrived at that figure. Everything is relative and despite his salary, belts tightened in the Mayor's household during the recession.

"No more new car every year," he says. More significantly, however, is the Stephanson's housing situation. He's an empty nester but, because home prices dropped so dramatically, he cannot afford to downsize out of a house that is now way too large for his wife and him.

Even at the top, the recession hit home.

Friday July 12 – Guemes Island to Spokane, WA

After stopping in Everett, I continue north on Interstate-5 to Anacortes, WA, the gateway to Northwest Washington's remote archipelago, The San Juan Islands. The islands are about an hour's ferry ride across the Strait of Juan de Fuca, separating the U.S. and Canada. A much shorter, five-minute ferry ride from Anacortes takes you to tiny Guemes Island (pop. 600). My longtime radio colleague and dear friend of 39 years is one of those 600 and I want to stop for a quick farewell.

Guemes Island is such that as soon as I drive off the ferry, my heart rate drops; the entire mind and body relax. The island is dotted mostly with farms. Jim "Stutz Bearcat" Stutzman and his late wife Jacquie bought ten acres on Guemes in the late 1970s when he and I worked together for a Seattle FM station. With a long eye on retirement they built a beautiful home that Stutz now shares with the marvelous Lizzie, his endearing Beagle/Border Collie mix. As usual, Stutz and I reminisce, philosophize and deepen our friendship before I really hit the road the next morning.

The other reason for heading north from Seattle and visiting my buddy is the route I will take tomorrow to Spokane.

The Cascade Mountains divide Washington State in more ways than one. Physically, they are the north-south spine between the densely populated western third of the state – Seattle and the Interstate-5 corridor – and Eastern Washington, the so-called "Inland Empire" which runs all the way into Idaho.

The mountains are also called "The Cascade Curtain" because crossing them is like going from one dimension to another. While Washington is called The Evergreen State, most of the evergreens are west of the Cascades. So are most of the liberals, most of the money and most of the votes. The late Democratic Senator Warren Magnuson famously said, "You can see all the votes you need to get elected statewide from the top of Seattle's Space Needle." It drives the folks in Eastern Washington crazy and they often talk of seceding, along with Western Idaho, to form their own 51st state. But, thankfully, this book is not about politics; it is about people.

I leave Guemes Island early this Friday morning for Spokane looking forward to a long, leisurely drive on one of the country's most scenic and rugged roads, State Road (SR) 20, The North Cascades Highway. It was completed in 1972. Before that, if you wanted to drive from northwestern Washington to east of the Cascades you had to go many miles south to U.S. 2 from Everett or further south to Seattle and I-90.

As SR 20 begins to climb the glacier pocked Cascades peekaboo through the foothills, teasing you for the magnificent show that waits ahead. Climbing higher, the road twists and turns between the now towering peaks on either side. Waterfalls *cascade* down the rocky mountainsides to the creeks and rivers below.

At Washington Pass (elev. 5,477 ft.) Washington State changes, physically, politically, socially and economically. Before passing through the Cascade Curtain, though, I paused at the pass to enjoy one of the most spectacular views in the state. Unfortunately, I was saddened by what I see.

Thirty-nine years ago, in the summer of 1974, I stopped at this exact spot enthralled by it all. The viewpoint is two miles from the highway and the resulting silence is a delight. In 1974 the surrounding peaks were full with glaciers and in that silence you could hear them cracking. Awesome!

Washington Pass Glaciers Today

Today, the glaciers are a fraction in number and size. If anyone doubts the affects of global warming they should come here. Still, the view is breathtaking.

Entering Eastern Washington the verdant forests of Douglas Fir give way to Ponderosa Pine. Cities and traffic jams give way to small towns, agriculture and vast spaces, empty except for abundant sagebrush and the occasional tumbleweed blowing across the road.

Northeastern Washington is both the fruit and bread baskets of the state. Just east of the mountains you drive through miles and miles of apple orchards and huge warehouses. At this time of year, as harvest time approaches, towers of empty packing crates await their bounty.

Further east the orchards turn unto vast wheat fields, much nearer to harvest than the fruit. You can tell by miles and miles of ripe golden wheat rolling back and forth in the wind. Now I know what "amber waves of grain" really means.

Before the final run to Spokane, I have one more stop to make, the legendary Grand Coulee Dam. This engineering marvel was perhaps FDR's greatest public works project during the Great Depression. At the same time, iconic folkie Woody Guthrie was paid with federal money to write such classics as *Roll on Columbia (http://www.youtube.com/watch?v=2sH6CcsTafw)* and *This Land is Your Land (http://www.youtube.com/watch?v=wxiMrvDbq3s)*. Now *that's* how to spend tax dollars!

Still savoring my daylong visual feast I pull into Spokane and immediately into the first Starbucks I've seen in 326 miles. While enjoying an end of the drive cigar and my grande quad latte, I begin searching for a place to camp. I locate two potential sites in Riverside State Park, a short seven miles from downtown. I know finding available tent sites on summer weekends can be a challenge and sure enough there is no room at either inn.

The ranger at one of the sites is Danny, a very nice young man in his 20s. He is sympathetic to my plight and asks the purpose of my trip. When I tell him about my project he becomes excited and asks if he can follow me on Facebook. I give him a business card and ask him to call me if a campsite miracle occurs.

As a backup to camping I've arranged the fully packed Jeep to allow Trooper and me to sleep in the back at truck stops or rest areas. As I pull into a particularly dumpy-looking truck stop my mobile rings. It's Danny.

"Hey," he is enthusiastic, "I found you a tent site! We have an equestrian campground nearby. I checked and they have one available. Head there now."

I know truck stop camping might be in my future but not tonight. Tomorrow, I will ask the people of Spokane how the Great Recession affected their lives.

Saturday July 13 – Spokane, WA

The sites at Riverfront State Park's equestrian campground have small corrals for folks traveling with their equine companions, although the campground is open to all. I decide to start my Spokane experience by interviewing my camping neighbors.

Looking at their campsite across the small dirt road from me, Spokane residents Jason, 39-years old, and Susan, 52, look to be doing fine. There is a shiny red late model Ram truck with a camper filling the truck bed and a trailer for three corralled horses (theirs and one for their nine year old granddaughter). Looks can be deceiving; everything was purchased pre-recession when Jason had full employment as a welder. Susan still works from the home as a medical billing clerk.

"It's affected me a lot," says Susan. "I make fairly good money but everything has gone up, especially fuel and food. Buying clothes is a necessity and that's outrageously expensive especially now that we've taken in our granddaughter. I feel like what I make is a lot less than what is reality. Now, it's hard to make ends meet; we are living paycheck to paycheck. It's very hard to put anything into savings. It's a lot of stress, a lot of stress that wasn't there before. I never had to worry about a dollar."

"What really hurts," she continues, "is that we can't go out on a date, can't go out to a movie or dinner. We never had to hesitate to go into a McDonald's; now even McDonald's is expensive."

For Jason, the hit was more direct. "As work dried up my hours got cut," he says. "Some days I didn't know if I get there would I still have a job? Instead of raises, I got pay cuts. The stress was incredible. If it wasn't for my wife's paycheck we'd really be under water."

In what would become a statement repeated over and over, medical insurance is killing Jason and Susan. They are paying more than a $1,000 a month and it doesn't include dental or vision coverage. Their beloved camping and horseback riding trips have also suffered.

"We used to go further north all the time," says Jason. "Now we have to save two months ahead to come here, just a 15-minute drive. It's changed me. I like to do things, get up and go. Now I just feel older."

Spokane is Eastern Washington's biggest city and the state's second largest with 209,525 people in 2012. It's grown since the 2010 census when the population was just over 198,000.

In the grand scheme of things it is by no means a BIG city. Its two tallest buildings are 20 floors each. Pedestrian traffic is light in downtown Spokane on this pleasantly warm Saturday afternoon. The streets in downtown are wide and free-flowing three-lane affairs unlike the crowded narrow streets in older, bigger cities.

It is a perfect day to visit Riverfront Park, site of Expo (19)74, the first environmentally themed World's Fair. Today it is a crowded 100 acres of beautiful green space and amusements along the Spokane River smack dab in the middle of the city. It is a veritable goldmine for post-recession stories.

Richard and Heather Morgan are 42 and 35 years old respectively. With two kids ages six and two they have a positive story to tell. Heather is what I call a domestic engineer; let's be clear, married women who stay at home still work, many of them also managing the family finances. Richard is a chemist and he says the recession actually helped him.

"I quit my job at the height of the recession and got a new job at a start-up company," he explains. "We ended up making a lot more money (Note the inclusive 'we.' Here is a man who respects his wife as a partner and I respect him for that). And, because of the recession we were able to buy a house for a lot less than we normally would've paid."

Richard's start-up company also benefitted from the recession, using federal economic stimulus grants for its creation.

On the down side, the Morgan's 401K took a dive, but not enough to offset the good news of Richard's higher income. The dive *was* big enough, according to Heather, "that we'll have to work an extra five or ten years."

Positive or negative, the Morgan's learned some things. "I learned not to listen to the news so much as to how thing are," says Richard. "I learned not to be scared by what I hear because you have chances to make money in a good or bad economy if you play it right and you are lucky."

Heather shares Richard's sunny outlook, "I learned that you have to enjoy life; go out and have fun every day."

My ex-mother-in-law, a very wise woman, would have called them "FPs, Fucking Pollyannas."

Heather's optimism, however, is colored by reality. "Groceries have gone from about $400 a month to about $800. It's a struggle to keep it from going to $900. Insurance is higher; we have to pay about $1,200 a month for medical insurance. Our lifestyle has changed; we don't go out as much. We don't go anywhere that uses a lot of gas. I keep a very tight budget now."

Did the recession change them personally? "Heather says, "For me, I think about money a lot more, I think about it every day."

The next couple I speak with has a different view on life and the recession. Bob and Susan Grey are both in their mid-60s. Both are retired – Bob was a software engineer, Susan a paralegal. Bob says he saw the economic handwriting on the wall and took steps to make the couple bulletproof.

"I knew we couldn't continue the way we were going (the royal 'we.'). I saw the recession coming and took matters into my own hands. I had an IRA and learned all I could. I pulled out of the IRA and invested, especially in oil. It's tripled in price since 1999. We just bought a new house and paid cash for it."

The crowd at Riverfront Park was an economic microcosm. From the financial security of the Morgan's and the Greys, there was the lonely frail-looking man sitting on a grass hill in the shade of a huge oak tree and the swarthy dapper-looking man sunning himself in the plaza – both jobless.

The dapper 46-year old Alex is a New York City transplant who lost his consulting business after the crash. His timing was impeccable; he started up in 2008 and had no clients by 2010. Now he's looking for work and living frugally on his savings. He recently moved to Spokane to live with his daughter and grandson.

"The recession changed my life," he says. "It sucks and I'm depressed."

Staring into space in the cool shade on his grassy hill, 55-year old William is stricken with a degenerative neurological disorder and cannot work. He barely scrapes by on a steadily diminishing state disability program strapped by budget cuts, hoping he can make it to 65 and Social Security benefits. Down to $190 a month, his state money barely pays for food. He lives wherever he can lay his head at night and has a forlorn, hopeless look in his eyes. "You will be in my thoughts and prayers," I tell him after our conversation. I mouth the words sincerely, yet they feel so empty; here is a man with little hope for the future.

Finally, there is Balloon Guy, the only name he'll give. Sporting a red high hat and wearing a bright, checkered multi-colored coat, he's sitting on a bench just off the plaza creating balloon animals for kids and inner kids.

He only claims 55-years of life but I'm guessing he's closer to 70. "I quit school in the third grade," he says unapologetically. Didn't see no reason for it."

He is more than functionally illiterate. "I can't read or write," he explains, "and nobody wants to hire someone without any education so this is what I do."

That is all he'll share. Balloon Guy doesn't want to talk about how much he makes, how or where he lives. All he'll say is, "The recession didn't mean nothin' to me," obviously unaware of the double negative.

That is not to say that Balloon Guy is stupid or some kind of idiot, far from it. As soon as I turn off my digital recorder he begins reciting a complex, intricate poem about life in the forest. His pace is fast, almost frenetic but the rhythm of the piece and the descriptions are captivating. He is done before I can restart the recorder.

"Wrote that in my head," he proudly proclaims. I am astounded. Balloon Guy may be more literate than a lot of other people I know.

Chapter 2 – Surprise in Montana

Monday July 15 – Spokane to Butte, MT

It's time to leave Spokane. I really enjoyed visiting The Lilac City. I've been here before, mostly on business, and never really had time to drive around. It is mostly a pretty place; the neighborhoods and their homes are well kept but frankly, downtown is boring and butt ugly except for its magnificent Riverfront Park along the Spokane River. There are few remarkable or historic downtown buildings.

My next destination is really Yellowstone National Park and a few days off to enjoy one of our nation's great treasures. Rather than a straight shot to Yellowstone, an eight-hour drive without stops, I will stop tonight in Butte, MT and conduct some interviews there.

I quickly cross from Washington into Idaho's beautiful panhandle shortly after leaving Spokane. I am driving on I-90 because there aren't very many other highways heading east in this rugged mountainous part of America. After crossing Lake Coeur d'Alene, a 25-mile long jewel that is a vast recreational playground, I am surrounded by tall peaks. The panhandle is separated from the rest of Idaho by a string of east-west mountains and, because of them the small towns and cities along my route hug the freeway without spreading too far in either direction.

After crossing into Montana about 70 miles east of Spokane I see a thick white column of smoke rising from a hillside ahead. At first it looks like a big puffy white cloud but everywhere else there is clear blue sky. I know it is a wildfire. Sure enough, as I pull off I-90 at Mullan, MT the hillside across the freeway is intermittently covered in rising smoke and fire units are gassing up at the truck stop. A water tank helicopter flies overhead after refilling its tank in a nearby lake. Suddenly, the white smoke turns a murky brown, a sure sign of a flare up or a new extension of the blaze.

"Some yayhoo decided to burn a pile of plywood in his backyard," says the woman standing next to me. "It started last night and quickly spread out of control. He ought to know better; this is the no burn season." I watched the action for a while longer before continuing on to Butte.

"It's pronounced "Beaut," not Butt. It's not boo TAY, nor is it butt TEE." This is apparently a problem. The barista at Butte's only Starbucks explains with resignation, "Most out of towners who stop here call it Butt. When I call the company help line the IT people always pause before pronouncing it, like they're not sure." I'm just grateful there's a Starbucks here no matter how you pronounce it. Are you starting to see a pattern here?

In case you haven't noticed, I'm spending a lot of time at Starbucks along the way. Yes, I'm addicted but Howard Schultz's free WiFi is also a major attraction.

One of the smartest things I did before leaving Seattle was purchasing a $10 U.S. National Parks LIFETIME senior pass. For those ten bucks I have admittance to ANY federal property charging admission. I'm using Howard's network now to find a National Forest campsite near Butte not Butt.

An hour later I am setting up at the Lowlands Campground in the Beaverhead-Deerlodge National Forest ten miles north of Butte. It is a misnomer; this is anything but the lowlands. Butte's elevation is about 5,500 feet. Driving here I crossed the continental divide at about 6,200 feet and continued uphill all the way to the campground. I am certainly above 7,000 feet – down sleeping bag tonight for sure.

Lowlands Campground Near Spokane

--

Tuesday July 16 – Butte, MT

I've been awakening early every morning – usually before six – eager to begin each day. This morning, as I open my tent flap, I am in awe; a herd of about 30-40 elk is racing across the field right in front of me. I am transfixed. They move too fast and disappear into the woods before I can get my hands on my camera. The image is burned into my memory; they are elegant and awesomely powerful.

I must rouse myself from nature's glory, however, and get my ass to work. I drive down from my 7,000-foot mountain aerie and head to town.

Butte is a small, proud city. Population in 2012 was 33,720. Its past and present is mining. At one time this was called "The Richest Hill on Earth."

The city was born in 1864 when prospectors discovered gold in nearby Silver Bow Creek. By 1870 the placer claims petered out and so did the population, dropping from 500 to 150.

The second boom, and the one that cemented the city's future, came in 1875 when rich silver deposits and then copper were discovered. The famous Anaconda Copper Mining Company opened for business in 1880 and soon after built the world's largest smelter. Butte was Anaconda's company town until the company faded into history after 96 years in business. All the underground mines ceased operations in the mid-1970s and more than 3,000 miners lost their jobs. Today one company, Montana Resources, mines copper in Butte, employing about 400 workers to extract and process the mineral from the huge open pit left by Anaconda. Still, Butte produces more than eight percent of the nation's copper.

Needless to say, Butte and environs suffered severe environmental damage from the years of mining. Surprisingly (to me, anyway), ARCO, which purchased and closed Anaconda in the 1970s, has spent more than $400 million on reclamation work to repair damage in the area by capping mine tailings with clean dirt, landscaping and re-vegetating damaged land. In 2004 ARCO agreed to contribute an additional $50 million to the Montana Superfund in efforts to clean up the Clark Fork Basin.

Historic downtown Butte reflects the city's heritage with many of the original red brick buildings from the late 19th Century still standing. Several are undergoing renovation. Street names like Copper, Gold, Mercury, Silver and Platinum are constant reminders of the past.

Curtis Playhouse – Built in 1892 - Downtown Butte

But, what would I find in post-recession 2013? In fact, it was what I didn't find that is the surprising story.

Downtown is very quiet this sunny and cool Tuesday morning so I head into some neighborhoods looking for interviews. My first stop is an Albertson's Grocery Store. The seven or eight people with whom I speak all have the same thing to say, the recession had little or no affect on them. I think to myself, "That's odd. I'll drive around some more and get the real story."

I want to see the old Anaconda mining pit and the existing Montana Resources operation. What can I say? The open pit is gargantuan and ugly. Across the four-lane road from the pit is a small, mostly rundown neighborhood of tiny single-family homes and small trailer parks. Prime interview territory is my immediate thought, disgruntled and unemployed mineworkers. Oh boy!

I walk the neighborhood for about an hour and speak to five or six people watering their lawns and tending gardens. None have any connection to the mine and, they tell me, neither do their neighbors. More surprising, they all say the recession virtually passed them by. "I was poor before the recession," one woman tells me, "and I'm still poor. The good news is I ain't much poorer."

Now I'm feeling frustrated. What the hell's going on here?

My frustration is short-lived, however, as I quickly realize this *is* the story. Did the recession really miss this small city? Time to talk to "official" Butte.

The Butte-Silver Bow government is combined for the city and the county. There is an elected executive, no mayor. Executive Matt Vincent is tied up in daylong meetings so I look for another official who might have insight. Community Development Director Karen Byrnes is kind enough to quickly return my call and even more kind to invite me to her office for an interview. I defer. "I am under-dressed," I tell her.

"I would be doing a disservice to a public official to appear in your office in my grubby on-the-road duds, let's just talk on the phone."

I am about to give Ms. Byrnes my standard "Please, no chamber of commerce answers" request but, as I listen to her, I hear the ring of truth in her remarks.

"We were fortunate; the recession did have little affect," she says. "The 19th Century mining booms brought a hearty and diverse group of people here and they stayed. And, their descendants stayed. They are hardworking, industrious and they never give up. As a result, when the Anaconda Mine closed, instead of rolling over and dying in self-pity we went right back to work and began diversifying."

While mining is still a big piece of Butte's economic picture, the city now also depends on several other economic drivers, like tourism for example. The many renovation projects in historic downtown are one example of the city's efforts to boost the industry.

Transportation is another factor. Butte is a major inland port from which imported cargo is shipped via rail and motor carrier to points throughout the Midwest. Butte is located at Montana's only rail interline of the Union Pacific and Burlington Northern railroads. Piggyback service is provided, and trains run up to twelve times weekly from here. Several motor freight carriers regularly transport goods through facilities in Butte, with overnight and second-day delivery to major cities in the West and Midwest.

Other major employers like universities, hospitals and the state electric utility (3,000 local employees) protected Butte during the recession.

So, if you want to live in the mountains with broad strokes of the old west, try Butte, MT where the median house price is $122,000 and unemployment hovers around five percent.

Wait; did I just give a chamber of commerce answer?

Chapter 3 – Bad Vibes at Yellowstone

Wednesday-Friday, July 17-19, Butte, MT-Yellowstone National Park-Rawlins, WY

My spirits are high as I head out of Butte, MT. I love driving through this beautiful state, Big Sky Country indeed. I am excited to see Yellowstone National Park. Established in 1872, it was the world's first national park. It's been on my Bucket List since before there were bucket lists.

I am quickly off I-90 east and onto MT State Highway 359 south, a two-lane blacktop with a 70 MPH speed limit. Did I mention that I love driving through this beautiful state?

SR 359 cuts through a valley in the Tobacco Root Mountains. This is cattle country with pastureland as far as the eye can see. Yellowstone Park is on the Montana-Wyoming border and the closer to the park I get, the more beautiful the scenery. Even though I am driving at 5,000-6,000 ft. elevation, the mountains are still breathtaking.

I pull into Yellowstone National Park at about 3:00 PM (MDT) and immediately see my first "Bison Crossing" sign. I love it. I use my Gold Pass to enter the park and look forward to setting up camp and exploring, only to find my campground is still about 47 miles away. The good news, Old Faithful is on the way. The bad news, I run into traffic, traffic jams and a car crash. Am I back in Seattle?

For a while, it feels like Seattle as I turn my engine off (waiting in a ferry line?) while the accident is cleared. Thirty minutes later I am on my way. The speed limit throughout the park is 45 MPH, 35 around campgrounds and the many popular scenic sites. Scenery-wise, the park more than lives up to its reputation but I have a bad vibe about the traffic and huge crowds of people. I've heard Yellowstone is jammed during the summer; I had no idea. I foolishly pictured Yellowstone's vast wilderness swallowing up the crowds. Hell, the park is 3,472 square miles but with all this traffic it feels like there are walls around me and they are closing in.

It takes me another 45-minutes to reach Old Faithful and despite the traffic the drive is exceptional. All the geysers, big and small, and related steaming fumaroles, are in one section of the park. Cars and RVs peel off one by one to view the lesser geysers but I remain faithful to Old Faithful. The smell of sulphur is in the air.

The parking lots around the world's most famous geyser are ginormous and packed but I am a patient man with good parking karma. Many geyser gawkers look for space in the first lot they see; I am more optimistic and follow the walking throngs closer to the main attraction where, of course, there are more parking lots. Sure enough, two rows away from the information center a van is pulling out of my spot.

And here I must rat myself out, shamelessly unrepentant. Old faithful canine road companion Trooper has one bad habit; he doesn't always play well with other canines. His first instinct is sometimes alpha dog and he'll bark, growl and charge. The last time he did this, he slipped out of his collar and took off after a Pit Bull. Since then he's worn an escape proof harness in which he can't hurt himself if he charges. The harness is bright yellow. Can you see where this is going?

Many people stop me and ask if Trooper is a service dog (because of the yellow harness). Until today, the answer was always, "no." It is 97 degrees here and I will not leave him in the car to fry and die. The National Parks are very strict about where dogs can and cannot go and I adhere strictly to the rules in the wild areas. In the visitor center and at the viewing area for the geyser, Trooper helps me WITH MY HEARING. The park rangers are gracious and sympathetic. Trooper is happy as can be and walks calmly at heel with a big grin knowing he's in on the conspiracy.

Old Faithful is really Mostly Old Faithful. Trooper and I arrive just as the geyser is finishing an eruption. A sign in the visitor's center tells us the next blow will occur in 90-minutes, *give or take ten*. I decide not to wait and proceed to my campsite, for which I made a reservation two days earlier. Good thing, too, everything is filled and I took what I could get.

Another hour's drive shows me what I got is what I call the Yellowstone Camping Ghetto. I register but before heading to *campsite #497*, I take a few snapshots of the "official greeter." He's a full-sized bison bull peacefully grazing on a small patch of grass just inside the entrance. He is content and nonplussed by the surrounding mayhem. I'm sure the Park Service pays him either $10 an hour or a healthy ration of something for the gig.

Lucky me; I get to set up my small domed tent with 499 neighbors, my nearest one only 20 or so feet away. The man of the van next door creeps me out. He sits staring blankly at the non-fired fire pit for much of the time. My bad vibes are vibrating louder.

I set up my tent amidst kids on bikes and skateboards, screaming kids and screaming babies. This is not what I signed up for (I know, ending with a preposition). I look at Trooper, "Ya know buddy, we may leave sooner than later. Let's see what tomorrow brings."

Tomorrow only brings more bad vibes, some my own stupid fault. For a few bucks you can buy a shower at Yellowstone. Let's just say Trooper was ready to throw me out of the car so I pay the price and another two bucks for a sandpaper towel. The private shower stalls form a row along the wall and I find an empty one. After a week on the road camping in the boonies, I must admit it's heavenly.

After drying and dressing I leave the stall and walk around the corner to the sinks to shave, etc. After a few minutes I realize I left my watch in the shower stall. I return to retrieve it – gone. I've been out of the stall for less than five minutes. Yes, it's my bad to leave it there, still; perhaps I'm too much of an FP (Fucking Pollyanna per the ex-mother-in-law) and I think someone will turn it in. No such luck.

Grumbling to myself about my stupidity, I head to the parking lot and the 17-mile drive to Mostly Old Faithful. More bad vibes; while I was in the shower house, someone apparently tried to break into the locked cargo box on the Jeep's roof. There are two big hinges, one in the front and one in rear of the box so it pops open on the passenger side.

Rather than try to break the two cheap locks, our criminal attempted to pry under the rear of the box and separate the hinge. He – and I assume it was a he – was unsuccessful but the box is bent so far in that it is no longer sealed. This could be a trip-ender; no seal and the box will take in water when it rains. There's no way I can fit all my stuff in the Jeep's cabin. Fortunately, I'm able to force the hinge back into position. The box remains bent but it is sealed. I dodged *that* bullet. But, that's it for Yellowstone and me. It *is* a beautiful place, if everyone would just go home. I've been in the park for 20-hours. I'm done.

I'm so pissed off I even consider blowing off the big geyser but how will I explain to my two mostly faithful readers that I was in Yellowstone and didn't see the big guy blow. So back I go to Old Mostly Faithful, get the obligatory pix and head for the south exit, 34-miles away and into Grand Teton National Park. Friends and family in the Denver area here I come.

Mostly Old Faithful, Give or Take 10 Minutes

Teton Park is different than Yellowstone, not as much traffic and much different terrain as I continue on the main highway south. Off to the west, the Grand Teton Mountains pierce the sky. They are simply spectacular.

Grand Teton National Park

I pass a few gas stations and consider stopping. Once the Jeep's gas gauge gets below the so-called halfway mark, it drops like a rock. It's dropping but gas in the park is $4.59/9. YOIKS. I do the math in my head; I can make it to the next town, barely, where I pay 3.54/9 for 18 of the tank's full 20-gallons.

The drive south through Wyoming is uneventful. It is mostly open space, cattle ranches and open range. I want to make it to Rawlins, just north of the Colorado state line, spend the night, do some interviews and head for Mile High Country.

I'm beat when I pull into Rawlins and, gasp, no Starbucks. I guess Howard Schultz figures a town with a little more than 9,000 people isn't worth it. Even worse, the closest National Forest camping is another hour to the east. No way I can drive another 60 miles.

There is a Kampground of America (KOA) in Rawlins. KOA is the Holiday Inn of camping with small cabins, RV and tent spots. Showers and all other facilities are part of the fee. Camping snob that I am, I'd never even considered a KOA but I'm finished for the day, so hooray for KOA. What a pleasant surprise.

The fee is $23.00, same as a National Forest site. Yes, it is homogenized and squeaky clean but I am home for the night. As a perfect symbol of better vibes, when I open my tent flap in the morning, a young deer buck is grazing about 20-feet away, his antlers barely one point. I freeze, not wanting to spook him and he poses for some shots on the iPhone. After my experience with the Death Eaters in Yellowstone, I think he is my Petronus. Harry Potter fans will understand.

My nephew near Boulder works for Dun & Bradstreet and we'd already discussed the economic conditions in both Montana and Wyoming, so I knew going in that both states, because of their high dependency on energy production, missed a direct recessional hit. On my unexpected return trip through Wyoming I will learn differently.

My sole interview in Rawlins, the owner of the only commercial espresso machine in town, tells me, "Between the oil, solar and wind power the energy companies provide most of the state's budget."

That's it for Wyoming, ranching and energy. It's on to Colorado.

Chapter 4 – Rocky Mountain Hi

Friday July 19 – Rawlins, WY to Superior, CO

I drive Interstate-80 east for almost 100 miles to Laramie before I can get off the freeway and turn south on U.S. 287 toward Colorado. Before leaving Wyoming, I see small oil operations and huge wind farms, reminders of the state's economic underpinnings.

Crossing the Colorado state line almost magically changes the scenery from the wide-open range to the beginnings of a more mountainous terrain. First small, then larger rock outcroppings appear on either side of the two-lane highway and soon the front range of The Rocky Mountains floats on the western horizon.

I always feel at home in Colorado. I love the mountains and the lifestyle. I've almost moved here twice. I'm headed to Superior, near Boulder, to visit my nephew, his wife and their two young sons. Of course, I will interview in several different communities.

Frankly, I must stay in the Denver area for at least a week. I've been on the road a lot early in my journey and gas prices are killing me. I've driven more than 1,500 miles since leaving the Seattle area eight days ago. That's about 83 gallons of gas at an average price of $3.70 for a total of $308.33. I'm not complaining; it is what it is and it's worth every penny. I am having the time of my life but I am on a tight budget.

Saturday July 20 – Louisville, CO

Louisville, CO is a 12-minute drive from my nephew's home in Superior. I'm here because in 2011 *Money Magazine* named Louisville the most livable city (under 30,000 population) in America.

"Top 100 rank: 1

Population: 18,400

Unemployment: 6.3%

This sunny, lively mountain town is safe (crime rates are among the lowest in Colorado) and easy to navigate. Lots of good jobs in tech, telecom, aerospace, clean energy, and health care can be found right in Louisville with more on the way. And there's world-class mountain biking, hiking, and skiing in the nearby Rockies. Real estate prices have barely budged since 2005, yet a typical three-bedroom house here still runs less than a comparable one in nearby Boulder. Its schools consistently rank among the top three academically in the Denver area."

Money's unemployment number for this hip little town attracts my interest, however. "Full employment" is technically four percent and Louisville's easily exceeds that. I am certain there are recession stories here, even in a place where the median home listing price is $383,569.

Louisville – you pronounce the 's' – is located 23 miles northeast of Denver. On this beautiful summer Saturday evening Main Street's many cafes, restaurants and bars are jumping, their large outdoor patios jammed – plenty of potential interviews.

Thirty-five year old Christopher is an electrical engineer at Ricoh, the copier/printer manufacturer – one of those tech jobs mentioned in *Money*. At first, Christopher insists the recession didn't affect his life but, as we talk, he admits it did affect his company, causing instability and anxiety amongst his co-workers.

"Many of our customers are banks," he explained. "When they got in trouble our revenues went down. I didn't feel threatened. If I lost my job, I was confident I could land something but many of my older co-workers were very anxious. Some were planning to retire in one year and now figure they have to work another ten. There was a lot of negativity in the workplace."

Twenty-nine year old Bill is a project manager for a general contractor. I seem to attract construction industry people like a magnet but every story is different, yet the same. Work with me here.

As the recession neared its "official" end Bill lost his job; the work just wasn't there. It took six months for him to find a new gig, at a much lower salary because he was "starting" over with the new company.

"I lost my job two weeks after my son was born," Bill says. "My wife obviously wasn't working so it was very difficult. We had to scale back tremendously. We couldn't afford to pay rent anymore and had to live with family until we could save some money and move. It was tough."

"We scaled back on everything, groceries, gas, where we buy, how we buy. Now, we've started to implement all the things that got us through, to make us more fiscally responsible for the future."

I always ask my subjects how the recession changed them personally. Bill tells me, "It gave me thicker skin. I used to be very happy go lucky and open. This just hardened me a little bit."

Shae is a 43-year old divorcee who is supervisor of the training department for a local business. Her divorce came toward the end of the recession and she went back to school for re-training. Today she is making more money than she ever has in her life. Shae tells me how the recession changed everything for her.

When the recession began she was a self-described stay-at-home mom with no income of her own. As with many women in that position, she was running a small business, managing the family finances. After the divorce there were times when there was no second income from her former husband and Shae worked two jobs while still going to school. (I LOVE tough women!). "With four kids, it was very scary at times," she says.

And, even though she is making good money now, Shae says the experience makes her "more conservative with my money."

"Before the recession, when I was married, it was house and cars, that was really important to me. Now those things don't matter; they're just metal and walls. I don't have to drive a Lexus to feel important. Now I drive a much more practical Honda Accord. I'd much rather go out and spend the evening with my kids, be with friends, travel a little bit. The recession gave me a better perspective."

Another single mom, 36-year old Erin Millikin, says the recession played a part in her divorce. She currently manages one of Louisville's downtown restaurants. Five years ago it was a different story.

"We were a dual income family, even though I was not working full time," she says. "When the recession hit, I had to take a night job as a waitress.

"Certainly my husband and I already had issues. But with me working nights and him working days, we never saw each other. As things got tougher, tensions rose. It certainly contributed to our getting the divorce."

Even in America's most livable small town, recession happens.

Tuesday July 23 – Superior, CO-Granby, CO

The Colorado Rockies might be my favorite region in America. Maybe that's because I'm here now but it's always been special for me.

I've driven through the Rockies many times but it's always been on Interstate-70 – nice, but not like this. Today I am winding my way through the mountains on U.S. 40 twisting and turning upward to The Continental Divide at Berthoud Pass (elev. 11,307 ft.). There are spectacular views at almost every turn as the speed limit varies from 45 MPH on the safer curves down to 15 MPH on the hairpins.

Rt. U.S. 40 in the Rocky Mountains

I am heading to Granby, CO in Grand County, 93-miles west of Boulder. I chose Granby because it is the largest town in a county with a per capita income of $38,000 compared to Boulder County's $52,000. And, don't mistake "largest town" in the county with "large town;" Granby's population today is 1,857, down from 2,080 in 2008.

While only 20-miles from the cabins and condos in the heart of ski country's Winter Park, Granby might as well be 20,000 miles away; it is the economic other side. The Great Recession came late, hit hard and hasn't quite left.

Wally Beard is Granby's Town Manager; he runs the place. His timing was impeccable. Beard started work on July 14, 2008. "There was still some building and things going on," he says, "but it deteriorated very rapidly."

While most of Granby's revenue comes from the sales tax, it was the property tax that took the biggest hit, down a whopping 40-percent and that's a third of the town's general fund, according to Beard. The town also relies on a "use tax," levied on cars and services not purchased in Granby. Beard says that dropped from about $600,000 per year to less than $100,000 now, a very big hit for a very small town.

Beard knew what was coming when he arrived in 2008 and immediately began preparing. He either cut or curtailed services across the board. Despite his preparations, however, the tsunami hit harder than his projections, especially for the property and use taxes. Miraculously, only one person in Town Hall was let go while another left voluntarily.

Today, Beard says Granby is a different town. "There was a lot of home construction going on when I got here and that has just about zeroed out. I know of seven businesses that closed in the past five years while four new ones remain for a net loss of three."

Perhaps the toughest part of the recession for Wally Beard was personal. He came from Bethel, Alaska to take the position in Granby. His wife remained behind to sell their home. Because of the bust, it took two years to sell the house. She was also six months from being fully vested in her employer's pension plan so she opted to stick it out. Beard didn't see her in all that time. "It was two years, 10 months and 15 days," he says wryly.

At age 66, Beard thought he'd be retiring soon. "Our retirement fund took a big enough hit that I'll be working another four years."

Thirty-seven year old Robert Cox has worked in the local Edward Jones investment firm's office for the past 18-months. Before that he was the Chief Financial Officer for a local resort developer. "When the recession hit bonuses went away, salaries were frozen and then we all took a five percent cut. Benefits started disappearing. Eventually, 30 jobs were cut, more than half the staff. In 2012, I was let go myself."

It took Cox four months to land the job at Edward Jones, not bad except it was a 50 percent cut in pay. He is married with three kids. "I've had to cash out my entire 401K to get by," he says.

"I went from the luxuries in life, doing what I wanted when I wanted to having to plan for things, save for it. I think it's actually come out better for me, a blessing in disguise; I appreciate things more. If I want something I have to work for it now. The other way was too frivolous, wasteful. Even if I got back to the old level of income, I wouldn't change anything."

Then, Cox shared an even more profound lesson, "I learned I was probably not raising my kids the most appropriate way, ya know, to have them learn what a dollar is, that ya have to earn it.

Kathy Burke manages the Edward Jones office in Granby. I asked her for an overall sense of how their clients felt during the recession. Her answer wasn't really a surprise, "Overall there was more fear and there is still fear now for another potential downturn. As a result people are investing more emotionally. If they hear something on the news good or bad they will react and move to change their portfolio."

Ski country never seemed further away.

I heard second and third hand about another Granby recession story and, it's a sad one but it's also too good a story not to tell. A clerk in an appliance store first told it to me. Town Manager Wally Beard confirmed it.

In 2010 a local landowner – let's call him Jack – found himself in a battle with the town council over some water rights or, more precisely, income from water rights. It seems Jack was experiencing severe recessionary financial pressure and the town was looking to purchase some water rights. Jack wanted, no, Jack needed that income. Much to Jack's dismay, the town purchased the rights elsewhere. As they say, payback's a bitch. Jack came up with a plan.

He took an old Cat dozer and turned into a tank. That's right, a tank. He engulfed the dozer in several inches of heavy armor, mounted a gun on top and literally went to town. Jack started by bulldozing into rubble several downtown businesses. He pointed the big gun at the local newspaper's building and somehow missed with his shot. Not to be deterred, he rolled on to Town Hall and, likewise, bulldozed it to nothing.

The police mobilized and prepared for a standoff and apparent suicide by cop but it was not to be. Jack's final demolition was, indeed, final. The rubble came down on his tank and he was trapped inside – end of standoff, end of Jack.

I guess every cloud, no matter how violent its thunder, has that silver lining. The buildings downtown are rebuilt and Granby has a brand-spanking new Town Hall – a beautiful building, I might add – and a new library that replaces the old one under the demolished Town Hall.

Thursday July 25 – Denver, CO

The State of Colorado actually did better than the rest of the country over the course of the recession and, according to a report from Chase/JP Morgan, its recovery is pacing that of the nation. Yet, Colorado's unemployment in 2012 still hovered between eight and nine percent.

I looked up these figures before heading today to Denver and the State Capitol. Unfortunately <sticks tongue in cheek> my busy schedule did not allow time to interview Governor John Hickenlooper, nor did I have time to return more than 15 calls from his office. I decide to "stakeout" the capitol's parking area early this morning for mucky-mucks with the hope of "ambushing" him. It's an old reporter's gambit. Unfortunately The Hickenlooper is a no-show but I am able to talk to some state employees on their way into the capitol building.

Even though the state fared better than most over the course of the recession, at its worst in 2009, Colorado was right there with the rest of the nation and my interviews reflect that.

Thirty-seven year old Rachel Fain works in the state's Child Care Assistance Program (C-CAP), a new position for her. Before this, she held a similar position with the City of Denver.

"It was just crazy," she says, "we went through furlough days, there were no more raises and a lot of the programs lost funding. Very early on about 10 percent of the staff was cut."

Rachel's husband was unemployed for the entire recession and all their plans came to a screeching halt. "We were going to buy a house and ended up stuck in the place we were renting. We stopped using credit cards; now it's debit cards and that's it."

She also echoes what is now a theme throughout my journey, saying it was good in a way because it's taught her children to "appreciate more what they have now."

"The experience definitely changed me, she adds. "I feel more responsible for my family than I did before. It used to be that we'd always make it through somehow but now the whole extended family is a lot closer."

Also passing through the capitol grounds this morning is 34-year old Lindsay, a writer for Denver's popular magazine *5280*. She says the recession only slightly affected the magazine, fewer ads equals fewer pages but her job was never threatened.

I ask Lindsay what she writes about. "Everything," she answers.

"So, then," I ask, "what was it like out there during the worst of it; what were you seeing and hearing?"

"I saw panic," she quickly answers. "People really didn't know what do."

That's understandable; even though Colorado didn't suffer overall as much as other states, it was hurting just as much as everyone when things were at their worst in 2009. My interviews in downtown Denver reflect that.

Thirty-seven year old Phil McCormick is an architect and, until the recession, that's how he made a very nice living until he was laid off. It took him 10 months to find a new job in a new field, real estate.

"How did you live in that 10 months?" I ask.

"I had savings," he says. "In one year I took $30,000 from my savings. And, I will always have savings for the rest of my life in case this ever happens again."

Even though he is single with no children, Phil does have a mortgage. He says, "it was very tough but I learned to never under-estimate the power of friendship and the power of love. I had people I could rely on; I had family. I will no longer take for granted the things that really matter."

"Still, I had self-worth issues. I sat around and watched other people get jobs and wondered, why not me? Why won't they hire me?" The battered male ego is becoming another theme in my interviews.

McCormick did get hired but took a 50 percent cut in pay.

Fifty-two year old Georgine is Director of Internal Audit for the Colorado State Department of Revenue. "We lost a lot of positions; a lot of people lost their jobs," she says, "none of us received raises and medical insurance went up."

"At the same time, my husband lost his job. He was a mechanic in the boat business. It was very tough. Unemployment insurance helped quite a bit and we cut way back on expenses. The whole experience made us much more conservative with our money. We already were conservative so we had some savings but it definitely affected my retirement. I'll probably have to work for the state at least three years longer than I planned."

Despite the panic and the caution, almost every Coloradan I speak with is optimistic about the future. Construction around the state is beginning to pick up and people seem to sense that the state's recovery is well underway.

I have two other observations about my week in this beautiful state. Number one, despite any optimism, just about everyone is looking over their shoulder and living like the whole nightmare will reoccur. Secondly, and this is not news, the people who live here absolutely love living here. I could easily live here though I'm not sure I could become a Broncos or a Rockies fan. Sports hate is so much fun.

Chapter 5 – I Think We Are in Kansas Trooper

Saturday July 27 Pueblo, CO to Dodge City, KS

Before leaving Colorado, I make a quick one night stop to visit a friend near Pueblo.

I leave the hot high desert of Pueblo after an enlightening and enjoyable week in Colorado. Last night I witnessed an amazing sunset and slept on a bed of gravel in Lake Pueblo State Park. It's either the gravel pads at the campsites or the rugged undulating desert. Gravel is better than rocks and baby cacti. Unfortunately, my self-inflating air mattress no longer inflates so it was a restless, sleepless night and I am moving slowly.

Sunset at Lake Pueblo State Park

I gathered some terrific stories here and enjoyed time with dear family and friends. I still love this state, might have to settle here one day. Now it's back to business.

I am driving east on U.S. 50, paralleling and crisscrossing the Arkansas River rather than super-speeding along I-70 to the north. It doesn't take very long to reach the vast wide-open spaces of the high prairie. About 25-miles out of Pueblo I begin to see the occasional cornfield and a few very large cattle operations, harbingers of the nearing Kansas State Line.

Looking around I figure this is certainly what they must mean by "hardscrabble farming;" the earth is a light tan, very dry and, I'm certain, difficult to plow. I can sense how tough it must be to survive here even during good times. I also gain new respect for the pioneers who first settled this unforgiving part of the country.

I slowly lose elevation as I near Kansas, dropping more than 2,000 feet from Pueblo's 4,200+ feet. Now there are many more cornfields, very large cornfields. These are family farms, some with newer equipment, many with rusted skeletons of older machinery sitting around. After a long day on the road, I drive into Dodge City, KS on what else, Wyatt Earp Boulevard.

First and foremost, Dodge City was a cow town. It thrived in the beginning when the Texas Cowboys drove their Longhorns up the Chisholm Trail in the late 1880s to ship the cattle by rail to Chicago. Today Dodge, as the locals call it, is all about Earp and the town's other famous lawmen (Bat Masterson and Bill Tilghman <TILL min>, for example) and one mythical marshal by the name of Matt Dillon. There is a Gunsmoke street, of course.

Wyatt Earp is one of my Old West heroes. Not the Wyatt Earp of TV and pop culture. That Earp was too good to be true. The real Wyatt Earp wasn't always the good guy, wasn't always on the right side of the law and was sometimes a scoundrel. His motivation in life wasn't always law and order. It was more about the money, either by earning a percentage of the taxes he collected as *deputy* marshal (contrary to pop culture, he was never THE marshal in Dodge City) or by running gambling tables in the saloons and sitting in a high seat with a shotgun in his lap, playing bouncer. That's *my* Wyatt Earp but that's not why I'm in Dodge City.

Wyatt Earp Statue – Downtown Dodge City

This is also Farmville and happens to be on my route as I meander toward the East Coast. I am interested in Dodge's current history.

In spite of myself, however, I am excited to be here. I will stay several days to also soak up the deep, iconic history of Dodge. How can one *not* visit the real Boot Hill? In another life, I probably lived on a ranch in Texas or Oklahoma. Why else would a kid who grew up in New York City love the smell of horse pies? That's for another book.

Sunday July 29, Boot Hill, Dodge City

Real Grave in the Real Boot Hill Cemetery

Yes, there really is a Boot Hill here and, it is the original Boot Hill of the Old West – a cemetery for drifters, bad guys and those without family and/or the means for a traditional burial ground. Today it is the center of the tourism industry which is about 40 percent of Dodge City's revenue pouring $150-million annually in to the local economy.

Penny is a 63-year old native of Dodge. She tends bar at the replica Long Branch Saloon on Boot Hill. She says Dodge City is a mixed economic bag. She explains there's been a long drought that predates the recession and it's affecting agriculture.

Seventy-year old Sally Brim has run the old ice cream parlor on Boot Hill for 12-years. She tells me before the recession they'd see about 90,000 visitors a year. Recently, she says, it's dropped by about 20,000-30,000, a figure confirmed by the local visitors and convention bureau.

It's taken a personal toll as well. "Grocery prices have doubled," says Sally, "and because I live about 20-miles away gas prices have been especially rough."

As an ironic and dry side note, Trooper and I are staying at the "Water Sports Campground," a very nice, clean and quiet place but I call it the "Non-Water Sports Campground." It used to sit on the shore of a large sparkling lake. Now it sits on the edge of a large drought-driven expanse of wild brush.

Non-Lake at Non-Water Sports Campground

Monday July 29, Just Outside of Dodge City

Agriculture makes up the lion's share of surrounding Ford County's economy and today I am driving the brown dirt section roads that divide the fields, mostly corn and milo, not too far outside of Dodge (sorghum, also called milo, is a crop raised for cattle feed). I want to interview the farmers.

There was a steady rain last night – not enough to affect the drought but enough to turn parts of these roads soft and slippery. I am using four-wheel drive and the Jeep finally looks like a mud-splattered on-and-off-the-road rig. But, what is this city dude thinking? While I am getting a feel for the countryside outside of Dodge, there is nary a farmer in sight; they are all out working the fields. I need another source of information on the state of the agricultural economy. Surprisingly, I find the source back in town.

Brian Brower has run the feed department for Pride Ag Resources in Dodge for 17-years. The feed store is dwarfed by Pride Ag's main business, a monumental white 1.8-million bushel grain elevator sitting just across the way.

Brower says the company buys about $12-million worth of grain per year – corn, soybeans, milo and wheat – and re-sells it to millers across the region.

"Even with the drought and the recession," he says, "we've stayed pretty decent but we're just now starting to see the affects of both on our economy." He explains that agriculture usually runs about two or more years behind the rest of the economy and bad times are just getting here.

"People aren't buying near as much feed, there isn't as much livestock as there was even a year ago. With grain for example, this year we are taking in half of what we normally do in the wheat crop. So we are now starting to feel the affects of the recession."

Brower also runs a small cattle farm outside of town. "Like a lot of cattle ranchers, I'm considering whether or not it's worth it to keep on going."

Texas Longhorn Statue, Downtown Dodge City

Tuesday July 30 – Dodge City to Fredonia, KS

The 240-mile drive from Dodge City to Fredonia, KS is straightforward, with the emphasis on straight. Except for a few gentle curves, U.S. Rt. 400 is a straight shot across the flat terrain of Kansas. Cornfields and small towns whiz by while the skyline is dotted with tall grain elevators

If you're a film buff or a Marx Brothers fan, Fredonia is the mythical country in Duck Soup. If you're a geography pundit, Fredonia is the name for a surprising number of small towns across America. If you live in southeast Kansas, Fredonia is an economic desert in the middle of a farming oasis.

About 97 miles east of Wichita, Fredonia is enough off the beaten path that the recession almost passed it by. Unfortunately, *almost* is the key word; the recession changed its mind and came back with a vengeance starting about two years ago. Its location a few miles south of U.S. 400 works against Fredonia's recovery.

Small rural towns like Fredonia often depend upon agriculture and local industry to fuel their economy – not so in this Fredonia. Location and nature conspire against this town of 2,480. That population number, by the way, is down almost five percent from the 2000 census and there are those who say it is still dropping.

I call this stricken town a desert in an oasis because the farmers and cattle ranchers just outside of Fredonia are thriving. The problem is they don't spend their profits here; they buy most of their equipment and supplies in the nearby larger towns that sit along major transportation routes.

I won't identify my source for the above – and following – information because it might hurt his standing amongst his peers. In a major media market he'd be called "a well-placed source." I'll call him Tom.

"Don't believe a word those farm boys say," Tom says, "they'll always tell you they're starving. Hell, we just had the best wheat crop *ever*."

He quickly turns to an old adding machine sitting on the table and his fingers fly across the keys. "Prices are strong. Ya get $15.00 for a bushel of soybeans. Let's say ya have 40 bushels of beans, that's $600.00 an acre and it may cost him $300.00 an acre. Say ya got 2,000 acres of soybeans, ya made $600,000 on your soybeans." A small fraction of that money makes it to Fredonia.

Record flooding in late spring 2007 tortured southeast Kansas, washing the region's economy away. Recovery almost came in 2009 with a small boomlet but the rest of the country was in the deepest throes of the recession and things merely leveled off here. One by one, local communities fought back, helped by their agricultural strength and rebounding local industries but fate was not kind to Fredonia. The cement plant, the towns largest industry and employer (90 jobs), closed in 2011 after more than a century in business. Ninety lost jobs in a town this size is a significant hit. That's when the recession turned around and swept into Fredonia.

One sign of how an economy is doing is sales of big-ticket items like appliances. Jack Studebaker owns the only appliance store in town, specializing in air-conditioning and heating. Over the last year, he says, sales have dropped 30 percent.

"I've always been conservative," he tells me, "savin' for that rainy day. Looks like it may start rainin."

There are no big box stores in Fredonia and few franchise businesses, save for the fast food places near the highway and downtown tells the tale. Almost every other store on every block is closed and empty. The downtown streets are eerily quiet, almost bare. Interestingly, just after the 2007 floods, unemployment in Fredonia was a miniscule two-point-nine percent. Today it is a few ticks over nine percent.

Two Empty Stores – Downtown Fredonia

There is some optimism glimmering around the clouds but it is guarded. An oil production company came into town about a year ago with plans for new drilling. Since they arrived, they've built a large headquarters outside of town, employing local construction workers and, with the people they've brought in, pumped more than $500,000.00 into the Fredonia economy in the last nine-months, according to Chad Estes, Senior Vice President at the National Bank & Trust.

Just Outside of Fredonia, a Derrick Waits for Some Oil to Pump

Estes warns, however, "This place was drilled for oil years ago and a lot of the old-timers say if there was anything left, they would've gone out and got it. This outfit has a new process, though. Maybe…" And, he leaves the sentence hanging. In the meantime, the recession still tortures Fredonia.

That's not to say that everyone is hurting here. Indeed, there are blocks and blocks of very nice houses, some of them very large and all of them well kept. Alas, there are many For Sale signs. Estes also points out, "There are a lot of dilapidated homes in town that need to be torn down."

Lee Somerstein

Fredonia Home: A Real Estate Oasis in the Desert

How bad are things in Fredonia? Thirty-six year old Amy Booth is the children's pastor at Fredonia's First Assembly of God Church. As such, she also deals with families and has a strong sense of what's going on in the community. "I've seen a decline for several years but last year it accelerated and I can tell this year will be worse" she says.

"We send out our vans to pick up kids every day to feed them, not just church kids. We can see that family life is changing. It's not uncommon for the kids to have one or both parents in jail; thievery is on the upswing. I see more abuse and neglect with the children, a lack of discipline."

"The schools are stepping in and also feeding families, as are the churches. The number of families we feed each week has almost doubled. And, families are leaving town. Over the last few years we've lost 25% of our congregation."

This all takes a personal toll on Pastor Amy. "I'm just waiting on the Lord," she says. "God works miracles. I'm ready to see Him provide and I pray all the time. More and more, though, when I pray I am also crying. "

Chapter 6 – Ozark Mountain Daredevil

Friday August 2 – Fredonia, KS to Lebanon, MO

I have mixed feelings about leaving Fredonia, KS. While theirs is a very sad situation, I met some nice people who shared very intimate stories and feelings. One thing I am learning (or reaffirming) on my journey, however, is that we Americans are a very resilient lot. Even in a town that is clearly withering away, there is hope amidst the wreckage. My kind thoughts will always be with the Fightin' Fredonians.

U.S. 400 continues on a straight-line east from Fredonia, cornfields and other crops still lining the two-lane highway. As I enter Missouri, The U.S. route suddenly ends and I am on State Highway 171. My GPS quickly routes me south on a narrow road with no shoulders. I suspect it is a county road but GPS identifies it as State Highway M.

I haven't seen anything resembling a town for many miles. I ride Highway M with cattle and crops on either side or the occasional farmhouse along the way. I finally hit U.S. 160 east, which quickly brings me onto I-44 and into Lebanon, MO. What a long strange trip it's been. It will only get stranger in Lebanon.

Saturday August 3-Tuesday August 6 – Lebanon and Laclede County, MO

There are 33 churches listed in the *Lebanon Daily Record*. That adds up to approximately one church for every 424 people in this town of 14,500. I raise this point because as I drive along Jefferson Avenue through the heart of town and then northwest into rural Laclede County both sides of the road are dotted with bible quotes on small signs a la Barbasol and many more on large billboards. I loosen my Bible belt to make room for them all.

The Baptists dominate with 44 percent of all local churchgoers. There's the Community Baptist Church (very large), the smaller First Baptist Church *and* the smaller still Second Baptist Church. There's no Third Baptist Church yet.

Lebanon's Community Baptist Church

It appears the recession hit Lebanon beginning in 2007. The hit was dramatic and got worse if you look at single family new construction permits (According to city-data.com):

- 2006   71 permits
- 2007   37
- 2008   25
- 2009   18
- 2010   18
- 2011   6.

Manufacturing is the big economic driver. Lebanon is the nation's largest producer of aluminum fishing and pleasure boats. As a result, metal fabrication also plays a significant role. The largest employer, however, is Emerson Climate Technologies (air conditioning). Agriculture accounts for only about five percent of the local economy.

In late 2010, as the recession deepened here, Emerson temporarily laid off nearly a third of its workforce that normally peaks at about 1,100 in full production. Overall unemployment is still in double digits.

Another key sector is transportation. Thirty-five year old Nathan is a supervisor for Conway Freight. He voluntarily left a job in 2010 as driver for a moving company to land this much better position. "They were looking for guys with degrees or who were veterans and I'm both," he says.

"But I can see the results of the recession with our customers. Nobody is hiring and we're moving less freight. Last year we moved about 350,000 pounds and that's down to 250,000 this year."

Thirty-eight year old John Simon used to manage a retail store but when he was moved down to a sales position as the company tightened up he quit and went back to school. "I went from bein' able to do anything I want to clipping coupons out of the Sunday paper," he says. Now, I work part time selling for the Mars Candy Company so I can pay for school. I'm just scrapin' by. I used to go huntin' and fishin' just for fun. It's still fun but now it also puts food on the table."

Joyce Fritzy is 60, out of work and living on disability benefits. She used to work for a company that made seats for Chrysler but she says, "They closed down and moved to Canada."

"My income went down by $30,000 a year. My husband is retired and he's got a pension but not a very good one. We don't spend money on *anything* unless we have to. Our kids are grownup but they're havin' trouble payin' bills and we can't help 'em."

"So, what have you learned from all of this?" I ask.

Without missing a beat, she says, "We're all gettin' older and we're all goin' broke."

Lebanon, Missouri is in The Ozarks – Hillbilly Country. The Ozarks are called "mountains" but, in reality, the region is actually a large plateau of green, rolling hills running through southwest Missouri and northwest Arkansas. The tallest 'mountains" are about 2,500 feet.

I use the term "hillbilly" gently; it is often considered derogatory. Technically, hillbilly actually refers to "people in any poor mountainous region but is especially associated with Appalachia and The Ozarks." According to Wikipedia.com:

"Origins of the term "hillbilly" are obscure. According to Anthony Harkins in *Hillbilly: A Cultural History of an American Icon*, the term first appeared in print in a 1900 *New York Journal* article, with the definition: 'a Hill-Billie is a free and untrammeled white citizen of Alabama, who lives in the hills, has no means to speak of, dresses as he can, talks as he pleases, drinks whiskey when he gets it, and fires off his revolver as the fancy takes him.'"

Yet, the term is iconic in American culture and has lost some of its negativity. Hillbilly Music is resurgent, especially with the likes of banjo-playing Steve Martin winning Grammys, touring and recording popular albums.

Driving west on Missouri 64 and away from Lebanon I spot a dirt road heading south into the woods. I take the left turn. The road runs several miles up and down hills, in and out of thick forest and connecting with a network of more dirt roads in all directions. Surprisingly, the scenery runs the gamut from abandoned cars and equipment and many worn out, tired looking trailers to a couple of large farms and one shiny new home that would fit nicely in any suburban development.

Things are very quiet back here but about four miles from the highway I see a man, his wife and small daughter emerge from a trailer. James Andrews is a 51-year old farmer/rancher. He leases a few acres to raise a variety of crops and run a small herd of beef cattle.

Andrews' Home – Way Back in the Hills, LaClede County Near Lebanon, MO

"Everything just gets out of whack," he says with a distinctive twang. "Everything goes up, fertilizer gets high, prices go up in the stores and beef prices are still low. Ya can't sell nuthin' right now, nobody ain't got no money so ya just keep the crops and feed the cattle."

"How does this affect your personal financing?" I ask.

"Well, it changes everything. Insurance is getting higher, gas is high and diesel is high. I barely get by just stayin' at home."

Having James recession story, I step onto what may be a slippery slope. "I want to ask you a stupid out-of-stater's question," I begin tentatively. "It's about the word hillbilly. I've heard it could be negative to some people....."

James cuts in right there, "Oh, it don't bother me none."

Emboldened, I query, "Are you a hillbilly?"

"Well, I guess I'm hillbilly as anybody else," he says.

"Can you define the word hillbilly for me?"

"Kinda like what we are out here. We just stay in the country and mind our own business and do our own thing. Everybody says we talk a little different, I don't know if we do or not."

They do.

Wednesday August 7 – Laclede County, MO

I wrote the above early this morning – thought I was done but the adventure evolves. Unbeknownst to me the Laclede County Sheriff's Department is looking for me, has been for the past four days. The manhunt ended with my "apprehension" a short time ago. While I had no idea of the manhunt's scope, I wasn't really that surprised.

It began four days ago when I was first haunting the back roads looking for hillbillies. You saw my sole success above, James Andrews. I initially passed Andrews' trailer and drove another quarter mile or so before I could turn around. Along the way a blonde woman, dressed in a red workout outfit, was power walking in my direction. She waved and I responded in kind.

As I made my U-turn, I noticed in my rearview mirror that she was watching me over her shoulder. Can't say that I blame her – strange vehicle, out-of-state plates, a big cargo box on top, starting and stopping miles from the main highway.

I turned into the Andrews' driveway and spent about 10-minutes getting my interview. As I turned left out of the driveway – toward the highway – it struck me that James used a term I didn't quite understand. Good reporter that I am, I made another U-turn to ask the follow-up question. At the same time, the power walker had turned around and was heading home. As I headed back to the Andrews place, she was now in front of me, still looking over her shoulder. I did consider driving ahead to assure her that I was no threat but I also thought that might really freak her out.

James and family were gone so I sat in the driveway for about five minutes and waited, futilely it turns out. I finally turned to leave and as I repeated my left-turn to the highway I saw the power walker stopped in the middle of the dirt road, mobile phone to her ear. I knew she was reporting my "suspicious" behavior. I considered U-turning yet again to explain my presence and again I rejected it; now it would freak her out for sure. I drove off and put the incident out of mind.

Over the next two days I was intent on getting some more interviews back in them there woods but it was as if they knew I was coming and headed for the hills – other hills. I did make another stop at the Andrews place, hoping for clarification on that one point but I never saw James again. This morning I made one more drive down the dirt road, taking pictures but I did not stop at the Andrews' trailer.

Heading back to Lebanon on Highway 64 I noticed a county sheriff's car heading north on a side road. Thirty seconds later another Sheriff's car passed me heading in the other direction. Glancing in my rearview mirror I saw him make his own U-turn. I instinctively knew why. "He's comin' to get us," I say to Trooper.

I've made it my habit on this journey to stay within five-to-ten miles of the speed limit. I can't afford a traffic fine. In this case I was spot on 55 MPH and a good thing it was; sure enough that cruiser was right behind me, blue lights flashing. I immediately signaled my intention to pull into the next driveway, a Conoco gas station.

Just as the older, white-haired deputy pops out of his car, another Sheriff's cruiser pulls in right behind the first. That deputy exits his vehicle and stays a safe distance behind his compadre, watching the Jeep intently. "Now this is getting interesting," I think to myself.

I quickly lowered my window, driver's license in hand. "Good afternoon, Deputy," I opened the dance, "I certainly wasn't speeding."

"No sir, you wasn't speedin,'" came the reply, "but we've had some complaints that someone in a green Jeep with Washington plates was goin' around askin' some silly questions like 'how many people live here?' and 'how old are the children, how many are there?' We've been huntin' you for four days."

That *did* take me by surprise. In fact, it alarmed me greatly. "Deputy," I said as reassuringly as possible, "I have been going around asking question but certainly not THOSE questions."

I immediately explained my purpose and detailed exactly what questions I was asking. As I talked, I noticed his body language relaxing. At this point, another cruiser pulled in. Deputy #1 still had my license in hand and I was determined not to lose control of the situation. "Why don't you go run my license," I suggested.

On the way back to his radio, #1 explained the situation to #s 2 and 3. They, too, relaxed and leaned back against one of the cruisers. A short time later #1 returned with a smile on his face. "You're good to go but if I were you I wouldn't go back there no more; folks don't like it."

I started to apologize for any trouble I might've caused but he cut me off, "Ain't no trouble at all. We've got an escaped convict on the loose and people 'round here are more than a little nervous. We've got to check everything."

Shaking his hand and thanking him for his service to the community, I had to ask, "By the way, just how many calls did you get on me?"

"Well," he paused to consider, "we got one four days ago, probably that walker. Then, we got several more calls two days ago and another one this morning. We've been lookin' real hard for ya."

By now he was talking in a much more friendly manner and I decided to take advantage. "Ya know Deputy, I've been wanting to get a law enforcement perspective on the recession. Can I ask you a few questions?"

He seemed pleased, "Well sure but I only have a few minutes." His mobile phone rang at that moment and he looked toward me after checking caller ID, "Just a minute, it's the sheriff."

As he walked away I heard him speak into the phone, "Yessir, he's writin' a book. Yessir, yessir. Will do sir."

Returning to my open window the deputy was back to official business. "Alright, sir, I've got to be moving along. You stay away from back there, y'hear, and have yourself a nice day."

This will sound funny coming from a Seattle guy but I haven't seen this much rain since 1954 when I was a kid in New York City and Hurricane Connie dumped more than 13 inches in one day. Of course, I wasn't living in a tent then as I am now. Last night I thought the tent was coming down, either from the force of the rain, the wind or a lightning strike. YOIKS!

Let me put it another way; this part of Missouri had about six inches of rain in the entire month of July. Between 4:30 and 7:00 (CDT) this morning 7.32 inches of rain fell on my humble domed domicile. It's rained off and on every day here since I arrived four days ago, some of it quite heavy, but this morning was something else and then some.

Torrential Rain Through the Jeep's Rear Window – Laclede County, MO

At the height of the storm the rain was so heavy, coupled with a steady wind of 25MPH, that one wall of my tent was blown in and touched the floor. The entire tent was leaning sideways. Trooper and I have been mostly dry to this point but at that moment it was if the tent just gave up and water started blowing through the fabric.

We've also witnessed considerable lightning this week. It was only a prelude to this morning; it wasn't merely flashes, the entire landscape was constantly aglow and flickering like an old light bulb. As the heart of the storm passed overhead the thunder and lightening were simultaneous. Have I told you how much Trooper hates thunder? The poor guy tried to crawl into my sleeping bag. I helped him in and held his trembling body until the worst was over.

This is also *my* post-recessionary story so I must pause here because I must pause here in Lebanon. That means I am halting my narrative – and my journey – for several days until my finances catch up with the calendar. I am paying for this amazing road trip with my monthly Social Security benefits, my only source of income right now. I'm not whining; that's my reality.

My money arrives the second Wednesday each month and while that's nice and predictable it's also problematic when there are five weeks between Magic Wednesdays, like this month. I am down to my last $120 with 10-days to go. Fortunately, I'm paying only $5.00 a night for my tent site. My cooler is full, my gas tank half so. I will hunker down until things stabilize. Luckily, there are only four weeks between benefits over the next two months.

Chapter 7 – From Noah's Ark to a Lincoln

Friday August 9 - Lebanon, MO-Springfield, IL via St. Louis, MO

Everything is wet or damp, including Trooper and me. It's time to drive, swim or canoe out of here. Checking weather forecasts to the east, I see that I'll have to drive well into Illinois to escape this unseasonable stormy, if not biblical weather. Fine with me. I'm so anxious to get out of here that for the first time since Idaho I will drive all Interstate Highways. Hell hath no fury like a driver drenched.

I-72 - Illinois

My original plan was for my next destination to be a significant location along the Mighty Mississippi River, a ceremonial crossing if you will. There's so much history along the big river and the economies are so dependent upon it; it is a perfect stopping point. Like the farmers, however, I am at the mercy of nature; I cannot endure another night of rain. Perhaps I'll have better luck on the westbound trip.

I map my way to Peoria, IL, six hours but clear skies in the forecast. As luck would have it my route takes me through St. Louis. I've never been there, always wanted to visit. It's a great baseball town and I have a good feeling about it with no real reason. It was one option for my ceremonial crossing of The Mississippi. At least I'll spend an hour or two there.

I spend about a half hour on the city's waterfront, snapping shots of the Gateway Arch and The River but my true destination is The Hill. It is one of St. Louis' best-known neighborhoods, a tightly knit very Italian area, always was and still is. You can tell by the Italian tri-color hanging from virtually every lamppost and many of the shops. It is also the boyhood neighborhood of a personal baseball hero and one of the all-time greats, the Yankees Hall of Fame catcher Yogi Berra.

Mississippi River – St. Louis, MO

Another reason to visit the hill, I haven't had a good cigar in too long and Google Maps points me to The Hill Cigar Shop. On my tight budget, even one good cigar will do. I choose a Nica Puro, the newest from one of my favorite companies, Alec Bradley, and I love it's rich flavor and bold character.

For the last week my meals have been limited mainly to fruit and granola in yogurt and peanut butter sandwiches. I ask the shop owner to recommend a good Italian deli for a Hero with wheels (No subs here!). Without hesitation he sends me to Gioia's and says, "Don't even look at the menu. Get the hot salami sandwich." Who am I to argue with a native?

As a New York City boy, I know and love good Italian food. The minute I walk in, the look and smell of Gioia's tells me I'm in the right place. I walk up to the counter, ignore the large menu hanging on the wall and immediately order, "Let me have the hot salami sandwich."

"OK," says the bambolina behind the counter, "what do you want on it?"

With no further instructions, I now have to look at the menu and the choices are numerous and dazzling. I am lost. "What do you recommend?"

Her eyes light up like an artist who just found inspiration. "I'll throw on a little Italian roast beef, some pepperoncini, our special St. Louis Cheese (combination of Romano, Provolone and Mozzarella) and horseradish mayo. You'll want our homemade bread."

"You bet your ass I want your homemade bread," I say to myself. I slum and added a Diet Coke ("No Pepsi."), all for ten bucks.

Before leaving, just on a whim, I ask her, "Say, you wouldn't happen to know where Yogi Berra's old house is, would ya?"

She shakes her head but as I turn to leave I hear another voice from behind the counter, that of a young man. "I live just two doors away, it's only a few blocks from here." Bingo!! The young man's directions are clear and precise; in less than two minutes I am in baseball nirvana.

She is sitting and reading a book. I don't know what I expected but it wasn't an attractive young woman in shorts and a college sweatshirt lounging on Yogi Berra's front porch. I glance down and the bronze plaque embedded in the sidewalk confirms I'm at the correct address.

"Excuse me," I call, "I'm sure you hear this a million times but I'm still another tourist and Yogi Berra fan. Can I take a picture?"

Yogi Berra Home – The Hill, St. Louis, MO

She smiles brightly, "Sure, go ahead." I snap away but I'm not done yet.

I walk a few steps up the short walk, "Listen, I'm sorry to bother you but I'm driving cross country and writing a book on my travels. Can I interview you?"

She marks her place in the book and throws me another bright smile, even friendlier than the first, "Sure but I only have a few minutes." I cannot believe my luck.

She introduces herself as Courtney Brown and then, my luck gets better. "I'm Yogi's grandniece. I grew up here," she volunteers.

"How many tourists like me stop by every week?" I ask her.

"Oh, hundreds. We get tour buses."

"How often do you talk to Uncle…..," I hesitate. ""Do you call him Uncle Larry or Uncle Yogi?"

"We call him Uncle Yogi," she says laughing.

"How often do you speak with him?"

"We used to talk to him a lot more; he used to come visit at least twice a year. It's not as much since he got older and my grandma passed away. Grandma was Uncle Yogi's sister."

A horn honks behind me and Courtney says, "That's my sister, I have to go."

Courtney Brown, Yogi Berra's Grand-Niece

"One last question, please?" My mind is racing, searching for a good one. I can only come up with, "Uncle Yogi is iconic as a slow thinking guy who never paid his syntax. I know he's not dumb; you can't be dumb and catch for those great Yankee teams. What's he really like?"

"He's a very nice guy, very funny, he's always got a comment to make about something. He likes to talk a lot. He never minded getting bothered by people for autographs and whatnot. Uncle Yogi now lives in New Jersey. He is a healthy 88-years old (Born May 12, 1925) and just opened the new Yogi Berra Museum."

As Courtney gets up to leave I can't help but ask, "Are you a baseball fan?"

"Of course!" Big smile.

"Yankees?"

"Cardinals!!"

So much for family loyalty.

Before leaving The Hill, I unwrap my sandwich from Gioia's so I can eat as I drive. I take a bite as I pull from the curb and my taste buds immediately scream, "STOP!!!" I return to my parking spot and my taste buds explode with pleasure. I was going to eat one half of the sandwich on the road for lunch and save the second half for dinner. Forget dinner, this is an unbelievable sandwich and I scarf it down right there. OMG!!

If you are ever in St. Louis, visit Gioia's on The Hill (1934 Macklind Ave, Saint Louis, MO 63110, 314-776-9410). Do not look at the menu; just order the hot salami sandwich.

I stay on the Interstate, my need to escape the torrential rains driving me forward. As I pass the Farmersville, IL Interchange on I-55, I am reminded of how agricultural Illinois is away from its big cities. I haven't seen so many cornfields since Kansas. Ninety minutes later I am in Springfield, IL under clear skies. I quickly check the weather forecast and it's good for the next week or so. There is no need to continue on to Peoria.

I find a county park with camping (for $15 a night!). I will drive no further but, Houston, we may have a problem. I quickly learn the mayor of Springfield is named (J. Michael) Houston and the Lincoln Museum is at

Sixth and JEFFERSON. I'm confused. I'll figure it out over the weekend.

Monday August 12 - Springfield, IL

Illinois may be "The Land of Lincoln" but Springfield is its epicenter. It was in this state capitol that Abraham Lincoln began his political career as a four-term lawmaker (1834-1840). It was also one of the nine sites where he and Stephen Douglas conducted their famous series of political debates in 1858. One hundred sixty five years later, Lincoln is still a rock star in Springfield. In fact, Lincoln-driven tourism is the city's fourth largest industry, pouring $388-million into the economy and providing over 3,000 jobs. That's a lot of dead presidents.

There are statues everywhere, along with the Lincoln Home, the Lincoln Presidential Library, the Lincoln Museum and the Lincoln Tomb, to name a few. I did not see any "Abe Lincoln Slept Here" signs.

Lincoln may be Da Man but government is King in Springfield; between the city, (Sangamon) county and state, it is the largest "industry" in town. Health care and finance/insurance are two of the other largest employers.

According to a study by the Atlanta-based consulting group Market Street Services, Springfield fared better than the nation and the state of Illinois in the recession. The study found:

"Health care, education and for all its financial troubles, state government, provided a solid employment base. Unemployment remained relatively low, housing slowed but there was no bubble to burst, and wages continued to rise."

Still, there are stories to tell from both tourists and locals. Richard is a 45-year old mortgage loan consultant from Chicago. He is visiting the state capitol with his family because he no longer can afford a more distant vacation.

"Needless to say my business decreased substantially," he tells me, "but it wasn't so much about getting clients as getting clients qualified for loans – people losing jobs, no income, no credit."

Richard's job was also at risk. "I've bounced around over the last several years; either my job was eliminated or the company went out of business. Luckily, my wife is a teacher and her income has been carrying us."

Nonetheless, the recession took its toll on Richard at a personal level. "It took away that pride and security," he says, "the feeling that I am providing for my family and I'm successful." There's that male ego thing again. C'mon guys, get over it! This is the 21st Century and it's okay for your spouse to be the major breadwinner.

Today Richard is freelancing, as he puts it, but considers himself lucky if he lands one deal a month. "I'm still looking for where I'll land next," he says.

Sixty year old Greg Schaefer has been a state employee for 39-years. He currently works in the Illinois Secretary of State's Office. Like government workers everywhere, he experienced a wage freeze, furlough days with no pay and increases in the cost of some benefits. With retirement on the horizon Greg kept a sharp eye on his state pension. "At one point," he tells me, "it dropped 40 percent. I thought I wouldn't be able to retire when I was planning to. I considered pulling out but decided to stick it out. It's starting to come back almost to pre-recession levels."

One of the most interesting stories I gathered in Springfield was from a young nurse at St. Johns Hospital, one of the two largest in the city. Nursing is considered a bulletproof profession because there is always a shortage.

That's why 29-year old Lauren *is* a nurse; she says the recession made the choice for her.

"It used to be that you went to college, got your degree and found a job," she says. "Today the degree doesn't mean anything anymore. A lot of people I know have their degree and work at McDonalds. In my case, the recession started right after I got my first degree, which was community health education. I applied for hundreds of jobs and ended up with one I could've had without a degree. That's when I decided to go back to school and get a degree in nursing."

Springfield's South 11th Street is more than just a street, according to Howard A. Peters IV, Special Assistant to the President of Springfield's Urban League. His office is on 11th in a neighborhood labeled as the 13th worst in the country by WalletPop.com. To Peters 11th St. is more like the Mason-Dixon Line.

"In many ways," he says, "Springfield is still living in 1960. East of 11th St. it's mostly African-American and low-income neighborhoods, to the west it's exactly the opposite. Many of the same problems, like segregation, still exist and some of the problems worsened during the recession"

At 114,250 people (in the 2010 Census), Springfield is similar to other smaller cities I've visited yet each city is unique based on geography, politics, economies and demographics. Springfield, for example, is the first city I've visited with a significant African-American presence. The census puts it at 18 percent of the population. Peters says it's much higher.

"During the recession Springfield's population stratified to an even greater degree," he explains, "Minorities from much larger cities like Detroit, Chicago and Indianapolis migrated here, mostly Latino and Black – some 'on the books' if you will and some 'off the books.' They've moved in with family members and many didn't participate in the census. I'd say the black population here is now closer to 24 percent."

Unfortunately, their recession-related issues followed them here. "Unemployment is still significantly higher in the low-income minority population and it only got worse during the recession," Peters continues. "Our rule of thumb is if the overall unemployment rate is X, then minority unemployment is X times two. For minority males, it's X times three. It is a devastating issue. Typically we serve the family through Head Start; we serve about 850 kids a day. Before, parents would bring their kids in and leave. Now, both moms and dads bring their kids in and start asking about what programs are available for them. We didn't see much of that before the recession."

Peters becomes more animated; clearly he is emotionally invested in his community. "There is a feeling of desperation; crime goes up, drugs, everything. We are making progress but it's very slow"

I see evidence of Peters' assertions just a few blocks away from his office as I am driving east of 11th St. In a small strip mall I see two men, each standing by their "ride," one a 1990s Chevy Impala, the other a more recent Cadillac – both waxed to a gleaming shine. Both cars are so tricked out they are almost caricatures of a Pimpmobile. They ride high on oversized tires each with big flashy hubcaps and adorned with assorted ruffles and flourishes.

I park at the other end of the strip to watch them. Within minutes one or the other greets what I assume is a "customer" who hands them something (Money I'm assuming) and waits while the man walks to his car, reaches through an open window and returns with something else. The transactions take but seconds. I've been around enough to know a drug deal when I see it. Talking about "seeing," I notice the two men eying me eying them and I drive off before their eying turns into something else. I'm a writer not a hero.

Chapter 8 – Getting Small

Thursday August 15 – Springfield, IL-Delphi, IN via Monticello, IN

My itinerary to date has been delightfully random and intentionally shortsighted. I usually select my next destination a day or two before leaving my current one. I look for smaller cities and towns, do some initial online research on those I like and throw my digital dart at the map. It's worked very well so far.

Yesterday, however, the request line rang and I had to answer; it was my brother Steve. His life is another book entirely but he won't let me write it. I pressure him relentlessly. Steve's story includes service in Vietnam as a U.S. Marine, an extraordinary career as a criminal defense attorney, his devotion to family, a phony gruff exterior, our shared terrible sense of humor and incredible generosity to those he loves. He is brother, hero and friend so when he calls and asks me for a very personal favor, one that would divert me more than 100 miles from my planned route, I cannot say no. I am diverted to Monticello, IN.

The drive from Springfield to Monticello is unremarkable. I have little choice but to drive I-73 East for about 100 miles with mostly cornfields on either side. Exiting to U.S. 24 East the drive is more interesting and the pace slows as I drive through small town after small town, their populations ranging from a low of 650 to an average of about 2,500-3,000. They are almost identical in layout and architecture.

Agriculture still reigns and I notice a new crop, a more modern crop. I am seeing some of the largest wind farms to date and I wonder why and how the locations are selected.

Monticello is a city of about 5,400 in north-central Indiana. It is a regional tourism destination because it is home to the Indiana Beach Amusement Park, Lake Shafer and Lake Freeman. It is also the ancestral home of Steve's ex-wife Judy.

I won't pierce their veil of privacy other than to say they did not communicate after their 21-year marriage dissolved but when Judy died suddenly in 2002, Steve travelled from his Brooklyn, NY home to her funeral in Monticello. Today, at my brother's request, I am looking for the

Riverview Cemetery to visit Judy's grave.

This is no small thing for me. I don't visit graves; to me, they merely contain what remains of the carbon-based unit that carried the person's life and soul, neither of which is present in the grave. I honor in my heart the people whom have passed from my life. I only do cemeteries when it is absolutely necessary and I'm not certain I ever want my remains to end up in one. But, I never say no when my brother asks a favor, so here I am.

Riverview Cemetery is at the eastern edge of Monticello. It sits alongside the Tippacanoe River, a tributary to the Wabash. Cornfields surround it. Even though it is 6:30PM local time, the cemetery gates are open and, with the gravesite ID number provided by Steve, I begin my search.

There is a brick home on the premises (haunted?) but it looks like nobody alive is home. In fact, it looks like nobody is home in the whole place except for the human remains and me. Surprisingly, I don't find it creepy to be alone in a bone yard. I do a couple of laps around the noted section before locating the grave right along the fence and across the road from a large cornfield. I get out of the Jeep and wonder, "Is it just me or does the silence in a cemetery 'sound' different to everyone?"

Steve asked me to more than just visit Judy's grave, he also asked me to perform an ancient Jewish ritual, the placing of a simple small stone on the gravestone. He surprises me sometimes; neither of us are what you'd call religious Jews but we both retain strong cultural ties. Still, this seems out of character but it is obviously important to him.

I bend in the pathway looking for an appropriate stone. Having never performed this ritual before I'm not quite sure what is appropriate so I look for something unique. Nothing, they all come from the same gravel pit so I just pick up the largest and smoothest one.

I walk over to the grave and stand for a few seconds. Steve, my brother the heathen, actually asked me to say a brief prayer. I do pray in a manner of speaking. It is part of my ongoing recovery and sobriety and my prayer is spiritual, not religious. Not knowing what to pray for in this instance I decide to just silently say "hi" to Judy, or at least to her bones.

A brief aside; now I am curious. How did that stone-on-the-grave ritual come about? It turns out there are several explanations depending upon which rabbi you consult. This is not uncommon in Judaism, politics or economics.

The explanation that makes the most sense to me comes from Rabbi Tom Louchheim at Temple Emanu-el in San Jose, CA:

"In former days one did not mark a grave with marble or granite with a fancy inscription, but one made a cairn of stones over it. Each mourner coming and adding a stone was effectively taking part in the Mitzvah (an anonymous good deed) of *matzevah* (setting a stone) as well as or instead of *levayat ha-meyt* (accompany the dead). Of course, the dead were often buried where they had fallen, before urbanization and specialization of planning-use demanded formal cemeteries. Nowadays one can no longer bury a relative in the back garden, or on their farm, nor may a deceased traveler be interred by the roadside. Therefore in our day one tends to stick a pebble on top of the tombstone as a relic of this ancient custom, and it is still clear that the more stones a grave has, the more the deceased is being visited and is therefore being honored. Each small pebble adds to the cairn - a nice moral message. This has become slightly spoiled by the cemetery authorities clearing accumulated pebbles off when they wash down the gravestones and cut the grass."

After fulfilling my familial responsibilities I head for Delphi, IN, a small town nearby where I will continue my research.

Delphi is the Carroll County Seat and checks in with fewer than 3,000 residents. It is located about 20 minutes northwest of Lafayette and West Lafayette, home to the Boilermakers of Purdue University.

Downtown Delphi is dominated by County Courthouse Square. Most of the town's businesses form the outer square of the square. I notice three women sitting on the courthouse steps taking a cigarette break. My first "victims."

Fifty-six year old Kathy is the zoning clerk for both Carroll County and Delphi. During the recession her staff was cut in half, leaving her as the only employee. Her job was secure but her son, upon leaving the military, had trouble finding work.

She calls Delphi a "bedroom community;" many of its small population commute to work for large manufacturers in nearby Lafayette. All three women tell me there were budget cuts and no raises for the last three years.

Thirty-nine year old Mary Ann, the deputy county clerk, tells me her husband lost his job as a welder and metals fabricator. "It used to be a big industry here but not anymore," she says. "He worked for the oldest manufacturer in Indiana and was low man on the totem pole. They're still in business but there aren't many people left working there. It took my husband a year and a half to find a decent job. Now he has to drive 45 miles to get there."

Forty three year old Laurie Brown is a secretary at Purdue University. Her husband works for the state. While neither was threatened with losing their job things have tightened up. Laurie hasn't had a raise in two years, her husband in four. As a result, they've had to slim down their living expenses and that meant eliminating non-essential luxuries.

Perhaps the hardest hit in the Brown family is their 15-year old daughter. She is an elite softball player. That means in addition to playing on her high school varsity team she also plays during the summer on a so-called travelling team. These teams are for the serious players and they travel to tournaments all around the state, and sometimes further. It's also a major investment for mom & dad.

"She didn't get to play travel ball last year and it was very rough for her; it's her thing, it's what she does," Laurie says. "It costs $600 just to get on the team and that doesn't count hotels, meals, gas and all the other travel expenses."

While the people I spoke with say the recession didn't slam Delphi, the housing market took a major hit. In 2010 there were about 60 home sales with a median price of $110,000. In 2012 the number of houses sold was only 35 and the median price dropped to $70,000.

Another affect is the ongoing deterioration of downtown Delphi. One man tells me it began – as it did for so many small towns in America – with the coming of Wal-Mart and other big box stores. "There used to be 40 viable businesses in the square; we had traffic control and you couldn't find parking. The recession accelerated the process. Today I'll bet there aren't five viable businesses."

The Empty Courthouse Square – Delphi, IN

Oh, and a side note; the nickname for the athletic teams at Delphi High School? What else – The Oracles.

Friday August 16 – Delphi, IN-Fort Loramie, OH

Indiana State Road 26 is a two-lane highway that runs in a straight line through cornfields and small towns again, with many beautiful old buildings on their main thoroughfares. Driving into Central Ohio, the scenery is mostly unchanged.

My destination is the Village of Ft. Loramie, OH, with a population of 1,478. It began as a trading post in 1769, set up by Pierre Loramie, a French-Canadian trapper and explorer. When construction began in 1836 on the Ohio Erie Canal – connecting Akron with the mouth of the Cuyahoga River at Lake Erie – many of the German canal workers stayed in Ft. Loramie. With the coming of the railroads the canal flowed into history, leaving behind a beautiful lake originally created as a feeder reservoir. Today it is part of a 407-acre state park, including a campground for your humble author.

With the exception of the housing market, Ft. Loramie seems to have escaped The Great Recession. Several large manufacturers, including

Dannon Yogurt's largest plant, surround the village. While hours were cut, few lost their jobs. What puzzles me then is the flop in the local housing market. Home sales dropped from 160 in 2011 to 80 in 2012. The median price likewise fell by 50%. There are price reduction notices on almost every For Sale sign. Twenty-eight year old Derek Pruder explains why.

Derek lives in a row of old homes just off Ft. Loramie's Main Street. He is a Loramie native and, in fact, lives on a block with three generations of his family in three different homes. "Do you have a permit to walk on my sidewalk?" he jokingly asks.

He turns serious when talking about home sales. "This house to my left has been on the market for four years," he says. "The information is out there, that with price reductions in Dayton people can get the same size house for $10,000 less."

There are signs of a turnaround. Out near Lake Loramie there is new construction of large homes that will sell for $200,000-300,000.

In my travels I've noticed a culture of RV travel. The huge rolling condos bring all the creature comforts to the so-called camping experience. I even saw a long, long trailer with one *outside* wall turned into a large TV screen.

By and large, while wave-at-you-from-a-distance friendly, RVers rarely congregate far from their campsite, unless they are travelling with friends, as is the case with the three sites next to my little domed tent here at Lake Loramie State Park.

These neighbors have RVed together for years and for the first time are enjoying it sans kids. All three families have kids the same age and they all recently sent their last ones off to college. After almost 5,000 miles and countless campgrounds, nobody but the person who took my money has said, "boo," to me, until now.

On my second night here, one of the women from next-door parks her car on my side of her trailer and comes over to pet faithful canine companion Trooper. Crazy as he is at home – barking and jumping on anyone who enters the house – Trooper is a model of decorum on the road. Comments like, "Oh, he's such a good dog," and, "My, what a calm, well-behaved dog," proliferate. I just shake my head.

He and Shelly from next door bond immediately. "Oh, we have one just like this at home," she says. And, in the next breath adds, "Would you like to join us for dinner? We have plenty of food."

I glance over at their raging campfire with row upon row of sizzling chicken quarters and a large ring of Brats. Reluctantly and with a watering mouth I decline, "Sorry, my coals are almost ready and the meat is out (my two scrawny hamburgers). That's awfully kind of you, though"

"Well c'mon over after you eat and get acquainted," she bubbles. Which I do and enjoy a very pleasant evening of company and conversation.

Behind my campsite, though, is the dark side, a pickup truck with one of those pop-up campers. It's a family of four although I'm not sure if it's mom and dad or grandma and grandpa. With them is a pair of beautiful Huskies and two small kids. The boy looks about six or seven, the girl four or five.

The first thing I notice is that the adults talk nicer to the dogs than to the kids – all lovey-dovey with the hounds, they virtually growl at the youngsters. OK, it's none of my business.

Last night – Sunday – the campground was almost empty and much quieter. Sometime after lunch I hear the little girl behind me crying. OK, it's none of my business – that is until I hear the woman scream at her, "Stop your fucking whining. Your not a baby, stop acting like one."

Well, first of all, the girl isn't far from being a baby and dropping an "F bomb" on a four or five year old bothers me. "Isn't that a form of emotional abuse?" I think to myself. I am sitting and reading alongside my tent and I can surreptitiously glance sideways and observe what happens next.

What happens next is that the woman grabs the girl by the wrist and drags her, still crying, into the pop-up. I quickly hear a quick series of 5-10 skin-on-skin slaps. It could be an over the knee spanking, or something else. I have no way of knowing. Some people spank their kids; I didn't. But, it is still considered legally acceptable discipline and not abuse. What follows is more troublesome.

"Get into bed, put your head down and take a nap," the woman angrily commands."

"I don't want to take a nap," comes the plaintive, teary response." The next thing I hear is one sharp, very loud slap.

"Take a nap!!"

Now, I make it my business. I can't for certain claim it is child abuse but I decide to report it nonetheless. It seems to me that last slap might've been to the face but, again, I can't be sure. I decide to let the park rangers decide; I will err on the side of the potential victim in this circumstance.

I wait a few moments – I don't want to arouse their suspicion – then casually rise from my beach chair and slowly walk to the gatehouse about 100 yards from me. There are no rangers on site but the staffer calls one on his mobile phone and hands me her phone. I make my report and surprisingly get a concerned, caring response.

"I've dealt with this before," the young-sounding ranger says, "and, I have two kids of my own. I'll head over there now and stick around for the evening. I often do walk-abouts and talk with campers. If I see any welts or red marks on that girl, I'll step in."

"Thank you, Ranger." There was nothing more for me to say or do. Interestingly, upon my return, the two adults had turned their beach chairs around so they were facing me. Intimidation? Perhaps.

I casually walk to the Jeep and take out the baseball bat I carry, not for baseball, and put it on the picnic table. There are no further incidents.

Chapter 9 – East Coast At Last

Tuesday August 18 – Ft. Loramie, OH-Latrobe, PA

Leaving Ft. Loramie, I drive a variety of Ohio state roads for a few miles each. The landscape is still primarily agricultural and it is still mostly corn. No surprise, not only is corn the biggest legal crop in America, we are the largest producers in the world. The U.S. Department of Agriculture estimates the 2013 yield will be 13.8-billion bushels, up from 10.8-billion in 2012.

As I go further east the history goes deeper and the many small towns along the way show their age with classic colonial buildings along their main thoroughfares. There is so much history here. I wish I had time to stop and soak it all up. This was the original "Northwest" as the New Americans began to explore their continent. Not only did they explore and build overland, they built canals to move their goods and they fought Indian Wars to establish new territories. Many of these towns – and their buildings – date from the early-to-mid 19th Century.

Finally I am on U.S. 33 North, a four-lane freeway, and the scenery starts to change. The number of farms diminishes and at first there are more groups of trees and those groups soon become forests. As agriculture fades I begin to see more – and larger – manufacturing plants. The biggest one so far is the Honda plant in Marysville, OH. It was the first Japanese auto plant in America (1982) and has its own interchange. Forty two hundred people work there.

Finally, I become slave to I-70 east. There is nothing but thick forest on either side and the land begins to roll as I near the Pennsylvania State Line. After more than 5,000 meandering miles and 11 states across the middle of America I am on the East Coast. I am reminded this used to be Steel Country as I pass through Bethlehem, PA. Those days, and many of the mills, are gone, changing the economies here forever. Some towns haven't fully recovered yet. I am north of the Allegheny Mountains but still, the terrain becomes rockier and I notice the overloaded Jeep is slowing more often as it climbs the grades. I exit the freeway at New Stanton. U.S. Rtes. 119 and 30 will take me to Latrobe.

Some people here pronounce it LUH trobe while others say LAY trobe.

Arnold Palmer always called it LUH trobe so that's my preferred pronunciation. I love Arnie. I chose this city of 8,235 people (down a little over one percent from the 2010 Census) for several reasons. Aside from its proximity to camping in the beautiful Keystone State Park, Latrobe is the hometown of two people for whom I have the greatest respect.

While I am certainly not a golf fan, I've always been an Arnie Palmer fan. Don't ask me why. Latrobe is also the boyhood home of Fred Rogers, the famous kid show host Mr. Rogers. While I found his style somewhat unctuous, I liked the positive and empowering messages he had for kids. But, neither Arnold Palmer nor Fred Rogers are the most famous *thing* to come out of Latrobe, PA. That honor goes to the banana split!

In 1904 23-year-old David Strickler was an apprentice at Latrobe's Tassel Pharmacy and Soda Fountain. Strickler enjoyed making up new ice cream combinations for customers and one day came up with a banana-based triple scoop sundae. The rest, as they say, is history. Tassel's charged 10¢ for the new concoction, twice the price of a regular sundae. Word quickly spread by word-of-mouth and in print until everyone in America knew about the banana split. Latrobe celebrates its most famous export every year in August with Banana Split Days. I miss this year's bash by a few days.

Only 43 miles southeast of Pittsburgh, Latrobe still has a very rural feel to it. Rolling forestland surrounds the city. Steel used to drive the town's economy. Now, there is only one large mill remaining, Carpenter Steel, and a few smaller mills. Steel is not even the largest employment sector in

Latrobe. Three local hospitals employ more than 1,000 people between them.

David Cullaney is 49-years old. His family has owned and operated the town's largest bakery for 65-years.

"This has always been a distressed area," he tells me. The numbers bear that out. Per capita income is only $21,393, $6,500 less than the rest of the state.

Unemployment figures and the housing market show the recession hit Latrobe the hardest in early 2010 and into 2011. Cullaney says, "At worst our business dropped about 20 percent. We provide baked goods for a lot of restaurants in town and along the highway; people just weren't going out to eat anymore. Our business was never threatened, though; weddings, baked goods for homes and fundraisers got us through."

Throughout my journey I've been looking for a law enforcement perspective. Other than my near apprehension and almost interview in the Missouri Ozarks, no police officer would talk to me – until I met Sgt. Nunzio Santo Columbo walking a beat in downtown Latrobe. At 30 years on the force he is the senior man on the force and he proudly looks like the quintessential small town cop. This is clearly his town as evidenced by the way he stops and talks to people in a personable and low-key manner. He certainly has a good perspective on the entire community.

Sgt. Nunzio Santo Columbo

"In 2009 you started to see the decline in business," he says. "The steel mills started cutting hours. The largest hospital had to sell out and the new owners cut a lot of services. They went from about 1,200 employees to about 500 now."

I ask Sgt. Columbo (He was NOT wearing a rumpled trench coat) what he saw as a police officer. "It kept me busy, I'll tell ya that, lots of overtime. We had a lot more property crime, people stealing from the cars, a lot of bad checks, drug abuse went up and we had a lot more alcohol related calls."

"More violence?" I ask.

"No, not really," Columbo replies. "We don't have a lot of violent crime here but people were taking what they needed."

Luckily, he tells me, only one position was lost in the department and that due to attrition.

Chapter 10 – Recession, We Don't Need No Stinkin' Recession

Yes, I am technically on the East Coast. After all, Pennsylvania is an Atlantic port state. I won't really feel it, though, until I hit The Philadelphia area and then drive up the New Jersey Turnpike to New York City. I cannot count the times I drove up and down that pike when I was a younger man.

I'm stopping later today in Yardley, PA, just west of Trenton, NJ, to visit my Cousin Roberta, the daughter of my Dad's brother. A few years older than I, she was my very first boyhood crush and remains to this day an easy audience for my uniquely sorry sense of humor. I can't stay long in Yardley; I'll have to find camping as I near New York City early this evening. The closest camping to the city is 35 miles south of NY at the strangely named Cheesequake (sic) State Park.

My drive from Latrobe to Yardley will be mostly on the Pennsylvania Turnpike/I-76. Getting to the turnpike is a soothing 45-minute drive along the lush and rolling state roads of Western PA. I'm glad it is so soothing; when I reach the turnpike entrance it is a rude awakening.

Even though I grew up in New York City, I've been in Seattle since 1974. Toll roads are a rarity in the Pacific Northwest but I remember them well from my younger days; they are the norm on the East Coast. On many turnpikes, instead of toll booths every few exits, you grab a ticket at the freeway entrance and pay accordingly at your exit. As a teenager I took the 90-minute drive on the Jersey Turnpike many times to sustain a brief romance in Philadelphia. In addition to paying the $0.31.9 per gallon of gas in 1965 the toll from the Holland Tunnel to the Delaware Memorial Bridge might have been as much as $3.95.

So you can imagine my sticker shock when I see the $26.95 it will cost me to cross PA on I-76. The next body blow is the $8.80 on the Jersey Turnpike from Trenton to the Holland Tunnel (under the Hudson River into NYC) followed by the $13.00 for the tunnel. YOIKS, that's $48.75 before the rubber ever hits a New York City pothole.

You may be asking right now, "Wait, what happened the Cheesequake State Park?" Good question; by the time I get there – about 8:30 PM (EDT) – it is dark and the park is locked up like grandma's jewels. This is a serious problem. My reservation in Brooklyn's Camp Gateway National Recreation

Area doesn't begin until tomorrow night. Moreover, Camp Gateway doesn't allow pets, which also irks me. In more than 5,000 miles, camping in mostly county, state and national facilities, this is the first that doesn't allow pets. I'll have to board Trooper. Sssshhh, don't say anything; he doesn't know this yet.

I have no choice; I must tap into my network of New York friends for help. I cannot ask brother Steve. He has done so much already to support my efforts. I have many old friends in the New York Metropolitan Area. I've known some of them since kindergarten! There is no hesitation to seek aid and, sure enough, one of my oldest pals offers to put me up in a hotel for the night.

I want to find a place near Steve's neighborhood in Brooklyn and as I search I find a new trend. High-end chains have built properties in so-called "transition" neighborhoods. Their room rates are far below those of the average New York City hotel that could be $400 per night or more.

I select the Marriott Slum – my name for it – near downtown Brooklyn. There is 24-hour security around the property which is surrounded by graffiti adorned, abandoned apartments and warehouses. It doesn't matter to Trooper and I; the luxurious bed, bug-free bathroom and large shower stall more than compensate for the view from our seventh floor room.

I get some of my best – and sometimes my craziest – ideas under the spray of a long hot shower. Tonight, as I wash away the last few hundred miles of bodily road grime, I am struck with inspiration. I'm not planning to interview while in The Big Apple. My plan all along is to concentrate on the smaller cities, towns and villages in America. There is one section in this vast metropolis, however, that I cannot ignore, The Rockaways in Queens.

Hurricane/Super-storm Sandy blasted into America just north of Atlantic City, New Jersey October 29, 2012. While not the most powerful hurricane to strike America it was the second costliest in American history and by far the largest. At one point Sandy's winds spanned more than 1,100 miles.

If you look at a map of America, New York City and Long Island are really off the coast of New Jersey. Sandy was an equal opportunity storm and did not discriminate between states. As such, both New Jersey and New York, especially The Rockaways, bore the brunt of the initial storm surge and made headlines around the world. Ten months later Rockaway is still rocked.

Before Rockaway, though, I have to secure my campsite and get Trooper into his Pet Hotel – they don't call 'em boarding kennels anymore. I had more sticker shock finding a place for Trooper, $50 and up per night. I was ready to dress him up in my clothes, cover his head with a hat and pass him off at the campground as my enfeebled great-grandfather. Luckily, there is a PetSmart in lower Manhattan with a Pet Hotel for *only* $32.50 a night.

Friday August 24 – Brooklyn-Manhattan-Brooklyn

Today is housekeeping day. I will reluctantly part with my faithful canine companion for four nights so I can cheaply camp using my National Interagency Old Guy Pass for $10 a night and visit with my brother and his family. Sounds simple, right? Nothing is simple in New York City.

I drive mid-morning from Brooklyn to lower Manhattan because traffic supposedly will be light. I am almost correct, except in downtown Brooklyn where traffic is never light. Nonetheless I make decent time. Now all I have to do is find parking. Hahahaha. I only circle for 20-minutes before I actually find a legal spot not too far from PetSmart on lower Broadway. I grab Trooper's file with all his current vaccination papers and head for the "hotel." Here's where simple stops.

"Can I see your vaccination papers?" the check-in clerk asks. No problem, right? Wrong.

As she is going to make copies, the clerk looks over the file, shakes her head and returns to the front desk. "I'm afraid we can't take Trooper," she informs me.

"What do you mean?" I ask incredulously. "He's current on everything."

'New York requires that he must be current with Bordatella (Kennel Cough. Uh, Pet Hotel Cough?) for the last six-months," she says.

"He is current for the past six months," I explain. "His vaccination is good for one year and he's had it annually his entire life."

"No," she says as if instructing a child, "he has to have a shot every six months."

"What?" I'm trying not to play irate consumer. "All his shots are current. Listen, I'm camping at Camp Gateway. They don't allow pets. The nearest other campground is 40 miles away in New Jersey." With a not-my-problem look, the clerk has the final word, "Sorry, there is nothing I can do."

"Crap," I say to myself, "no way I'm commuting between Camp Cheesecake and Brooklyn." I start mentally preparing to leave New York without much of a visit. Before acting hastily I decide to call Camp Gateway and beg.

Expecting the worst, I fare much better thanks to Ranger Pat. After listening to my tale of woe, Ranger Pat is beyond sympathetic. "I have two of my own," she enthuses, "Let me talk to the chief." After a few moments on hold, blessedly without audio entertainment or promotion, Ranger Pat is back with the good news. "Chief says it's alright. Just don't flaunt it."

What a relief. While I love seeing my brother and sister-in-law I am jonesing to see my niece. She is three-and-half and I haven't seen her other than on Skype since her first birthday. I am a sucker for kids, especially those with my blood running through their veins.

It is still early enough to avoid the home commute so my drive from Manhattan to Camp Gateway is a snap. Camp Gateway is part of the Gateway National Recreation Area created on Floyd Bennett Field, a former Naval Air Base at the south terminus of Flatbush Avenue. Before becoming a military base, Floyd Bennett, named for a Brooklynite Medal of Honor Winner, was New York's first municipal airport. It opened in 1931 and was decommissioned in 1971. I remember touring the base with my family when I was about nine.

Coming off the Belt Parkway at Exit 11S, the airfield immediately looms on my left. I turn into what looks like a main entrance with a big white arch. Strangely I see no signs either for the park or the campgrounds. Surrounded by playfields and long abandoned runways I drive along the wide runways toward the waters of Jamaica Bay where I see on an area map the campsites are situated.

There are a few small signs with the names of campgrounds; none of them mine but oddly, no campsites in sight. Finally, after about fifteen minutes of meandering I see a couple of people and ask where the camping registration is. "It's all the way back there," one answers, pointing in the general direction of whence I came. "It's in the Visitor's Center."

Retracing my steps by about a mile, I park in front of the obviously restored clean white building that serves as the Visitor's Center but, still, no signs mentioning camping. Inside, however, is the perpetually cheerful and helpful Ranger Pat who seems genuinely thrilled to meet Trooper and me. After signing us in, Ranger Pat unfolds a map and draws a red line directing us from YOU ARE HERE to site 39 just off Runway 24B.

Twenty minutes later I am still circling up and back on Runway 24B looking for #39. There are no helpful signs, no signs at all. Looking for the umpteenth time at Ranger Pat's map I notice that her red line turns to dashes and ends at a small side road next to the runway. At the end of the small road I see a battered and branch covered Do Not Enter sign. Having seen no signs to this point I figure this one is left over from the Navy days and I enter. A few hundred feet in, the road narrows to a path and dead ends with trees scraping both sides of the Jeep. I pull a nifty U-turn in the cramped space and slowly work my way back. This is when my day goes from Sunshine Ranger Pat to National Park Police Officer Asshole.

He is standing about fifty feet away from me at my point of entry, legs spread in a commanding posture and a hand raised in the air. Actually, he is a welcome sight; I'm certain he will guide me to my campsite. He will, but not before asserting his absolute authority over me or anyone else within the sound of his booming voice. As I creep closer I hear his dulcet tones through my closed windows, "**STOP THE DAMNED CAR!!**" I stop the damned car and lower my window, license already in my hand. "Hang on, I'll get the registration out of my glove box," I say.

Officer Asshole only speaks in **bold letters. "Can't you read the sign? It says DO NOT ENTER!"**

"I'm lost officer. Can you direct me to my campsite? I've been circling for almost a half hour." I say all of this calmly and politely. I am well versed in Traffic Cop 101.

Officer A. ignores me. **"That sign says DO NOT ENTER. You are in violation of the VTR."** The last sentence is delivered like Perry Mason nailing the lying witness.

"Uh, VTR?"

"Those are the Vehicle Traffic Regulations ('you fool' is the implied end of that sentence). Let me see your proof of insurance."

"Listen officer, I really thought that sign was outdated. As I said, I'm lost. Can you just point me to my campsite?"

"Don't you know how to follow MY commands?" His bold letters are nearly upper case. **"Show me the insurance!"**

By now there is nothing I can say that won't incite him further so I hand him the insurance ID and stew silently. This is new territory for me, *silent* stewing.

After I show warrant and crime free on his computer, Officer A. strides back to my open window, hands me my papers and in only a slightly less self-important roar, points down the now-violated lane. **"See that trailer at the end of this road? That's your campground just to the right."**

He turns imperiously to leave, as if he's just granted me a reprieve from Big Sparky. "Welcome to New York," I say to the back of his head, certainly loud enough for him to hear. Officer Asshole needs to work on his people skills.

Sunday August 25 – The Rockaways

Growing up I haunted the Five Towns of Nassau County, NY (Woodmere, Lawrence, Inwood, Cedarhurst and Hewlett) to meet rich and beautiful teen-age girls and to reach the magnificent white sand beaches of Long Island's South Shore. From my early youth until I moved from the city in 1974, I sunned, swam and lusted in Long Beach, Lido Beach, Atlantic Beach and The Rockaways. In high school my crowd's favorite hangout was Beach 32nd Street in Rockaway. Before obtaining driver's licenses we got there via the subway, The Long Island Railroad or BMT (By My Thumb). On any given hot muggy day five, ten, fifteen or 20 blankets would join to form our own ad hoc beach club sometimes with nearly 100 of us trading screaming teen hormones. We romped in the frothy waves of the Atlantic Ocean and patrolled the boardwalk, teeming with New York's ethnic potpourri and concession stands hawking great fries, greasy burgers, kosher hot dogs and a multitude of sugar laden treats. The rides and carnival games were a few miles to the west at Rockaway Playland, the poor man's Coney Island.

The warm memories are gone in a New York minute, or as Johnny Carson once said, "The time between a NY traffic light turning green and the guy behind you honking his horn." Standing on the boardwalk at Beach 32nd St. today is a forlorn, lonely experience. In days of yore, the crowds started building early in the morning until wall-to-wall blankets hid the beach sand. Now, the beach is empty and the ocean is much closer to the boardwalk than I remember, the result of erosion and storms. Instead of the noisy fun-loving crowd on the boardwalk there is an occasional runner or two and no concession stands. In their place are two almost permanent-looking construction trailers mounted on concrete footings.

Construction Trailers Not Burgers & Fries

I walk down the boardwalk for a block or two until there are no boards on the walk. Only their concrete supports remain, my first evidence of Sandy's wrath. I walk down to the beach without any visions or illusions of yesteryear. Reality sucks.

What Used to be "MY" Boardwalk Near Beach 32nd St.

With nobody in sight, I let Trooper off his leash to romp. The Golden Retriever is bred to hunt and swim after its prey and Trooper's first discovery is the unwelcome taste of ocean saltwater. With that out of the way he takes an introductory roll in the sand and goes off looking for a gnawing stick. As if from nowhere a security guard appears about 150 feet in front of us yelling, "No dogs on the beach!" Of course not. We make our way back to the Jeep on the dry side of the non-boardwalk. It's time to look for people and their stories.

A Typical Sight on Any Rockaway Street Near the Beach

Working my way west and driving up and down the side streets Sandy's legacy is even more evident. Rented dumpsters dot the streets while boarded up and abandoned homes sit silently awaiting their final destruction. Still, there are many buildings that look either untouched by the storm or at least their rehabilitation is complete. In other areas, entire blocks are cleared with new developments changing the feel of The Rockaways. That feel was created by decades of salt spray, sand and families in the mostly white mostly unchanged rental bungalows and permanent residences.

New Construction Along Rockaway Beach

Moving further west into neighborhoods with more homeowners I see lots of repair and cleanup activity.

The Tools of Restoration

Matt Quinby is hard at work swapping between a paintbrush and a broom on the front porch of his grey wood clapboard sided house less than a block from the beach. He defers to his wife Lee for an interview. Both are professors at the City University of New York. As a result, they were living collegial, recession-proof lives until that dark and stormy night. (Damn! I've been waiting for years to use that…).

"Sandy changed the nature of my classes," she begins. "So many of my students were displaced, they couldn't finish that semester or begin the next."

"And," she continues, "It certainly changed things here at the house. We lost everything to the water in the basement, the boiler, heater, the washer and dryer, etc. The most hurtful part of it was we lost mementoes, papers and irreplaceable photographs of the family. It was very difficult."

The Quinby's roof was also damaged and the combined financial hit was a hard one. "Insurance is hard to secure here and we had to pay for everything from our savings," says Lee Quinby. "We spent about $12,000-15,000 dollars to replace everything and we were amongst the lucky ones."

Becoming more thoughtful, she adds, "The whole thing made me feel more vulnerable. I've always had good things happen to me in life; bad things just don't happen….until this."

I hear many other stories this day, some similar and others worse. One man who doesn't want to identify himself is removing debris from his front yard. "We had to leave. The water was at the front door," he says, pointing to a porch where the door stood about five-to-six feet above the sidewalk.

"I am living with my son now and I come down on weekends to clean up. I'm going to have to tear down the house and rebuild."

"Do you have that kind of money?" I ask.

"No," my family will help."

The most harrowing story I hear comes from 54-year old Ramona Muño. Like the Quinbys she is less than a block from the beach.

"My home was flooded. We had about five feet of water"

"I stayed here during the storm," she tells me with a small laugh. "It was a little scary no, it was a lot scary. We left for Irene the year before and nothing happened so……. We thought it was going to be the same way."

"We're still recovering slowly," she continues. "I had to take money out of my retirement account to make repairs. I'll probably have to work three to five years longer now."

When I ask her how the experience changed her, Ramona Muño gets to the heart of her story.

"I used to think material things were important," she starts out. "When you see yourself in a situation where you think you might die, those things become much less important. You realize how much more important are your family, friends and things like that."

"Wait," I interrupt, "Go back. You thought you were going to die?"

"We were surrounded by water. We didn't know how high it was going to go. And there was a fire on the next block to the north. It was randomly jumping from house to house and we didn't know how far that was going to go, if our house was going to catch fire."

"Today," she concludes, "I cherish the people in my life."

Lee Somerstein

Chapter 11 – The Gods of Baseball Live Here

Tuesday August 27 – New York, NY-Cooperstown, NY

I am leaving New York City via its maze of parkways and expressways, Belt Parkway, Van Wyck Expressway, Whitestone Expressway and the Hutchinson River Parkway, on my way to the New York State Thruway. The Thruway – I-87 – is familiar ground; it is the gateway to the rugged and beautiful Adirondack State Park (2.6 million acres!) where I spent many happy youthful days at summer camp.

When thinking of New York, most people think of the city and they assume the whole state is like that but heading into Westchester County and away from the tumult of the Big City, the rest of New York State reveals itself, lush and green. The Thruway skirts the eastern edge of the rolling Catskill Mountains, although there is much debate over where this mini-mountain range starts and ends.

The Catskills are nominally 100 miles northwest of New York City and 40 miles southwest of Albany. Some will question whether they are really mountains at all; the tallest "peak" is about 3,500 feet. Geologically they are no relation to the much more rugged and taller Adirondack Range further north. Technically, the Catskills form the northeastern end of the Allegheny Plateau. Unlike most mountain ranges that are created by tremendous upheavals from below, the Catskills are considered a mature dissected plateau, a once flat region uplifted and eroded into sharp relief by rivers and streams. Whatever you call them, they are beautiful in their own way, one bright green hillock after another rolling together on the horizon. Of course, they are famous in American Culture as part of the so-called Borscht Belt where so many famous comedians got their starts playing the countless resorts like Grossingers and The Nevele (Eleven spelled backwards…don't ask me why).

At Albany the Thruway turns east, eventually becoming I-90. After too many miles of freeway I exit onto U.S. 20 west in the town of Waynesburg. The route gently twists through long stretches of forest, dotted by some fine old homes and the occasional farm. At one farm I spot a "Produce" sign and slow down; I am always looking for that elusive, fresh-off-the-vine tomato. When I find them, I eat 'em like candy.

There they are! I stop; make a U-turn and park beside the stand. There is nary a soul in sight.

I wait a few moments and then start choosing tomatoes. They are all perfectly ripe. I weigh them on the professional scale – four pounds but still, nobody around. It is then that I notice the coffee can with a hand-scrawled sign that says "Pay Here." At $2.00 a pound I drop $8.00 into the can and immediately reach into the brown paper bag to pull out one of the bright red beauties. WOW, it tastes like a tomato!

The road into Cooperstown is County 31. It is much more narrow than the state and U.S roads, the trees nearly forming a canopy with the first red and orange tinges of autumn tickling their leaves. The harsh winter comes early to Central New York; Cooperstown is in the southern part of New York's Snowbelt, averaging almost 70 inches a year. The *average* January temperature is 11° Fahrenheit.

A sharp right turn and CR 31 becomes Main St. Even though Cooperstown was established in 1786 (founded by the father of author James Fenimore Cooper <*The Last of the Mohicans*>) to me it's like the Baseball Gods dropped this perfect little village from the sky into the dense forest and called it their Valhalla. Apparently they also told the residents to neatly maintain their fabulous colonial homes.

Cooperstown Colonials

Almost immediately on the left I spot the National Baseball Hall of Fame

(HOF). It is a three-floor red brick building that fits nicely with the character of the brick colonials surrounding it. As an aside, the HOF is not affiliated with nor run by Major League Baseball. It is an independent non-profit organization obviously closely associated with the Grand Old Game. Before doing the HOF as the avid fan that I am, I have work to do.

Cooperstown – is there a more intense baseball town on the face of the earth? I think not. Almost every shop and restaurant on Main St. has a baseball theme. But even the Gods of Baseball could not avert The Great Recession.

Baseball Rules on Main St. – Cooperstown, NY

Thirty-nine year old Brad Horn is the Baseball Hall of Fame's Senior Director for Communications and Education (I want his job!). He makes no bones about it, "We have seen a significant decline in attendance since 2008. We've gone from about 300,00 visitors a year to about 265,000."

Horn predicts the 2013 numbers will be about the same. It is The Hall's lowest attendance since the 1980s. He attributes most of the drop to the recession, the rest to what he calls "environmental factors" such as Cooperstown's remote location, local prices (especially during the recession) and, oh yeah, that steroids thing in baseball.

Interestingly, Horn puts some of the blame on the people who run the Major Leagues. "Their emphasis is more on the here and now than on the history associated with earlier generations."

What Horn doesn't know is whether the attendance figures are "the new norm" or just a certain time period. Either way, it affects the way the hall is run. Even as a non-profit they don't want to operate in the red. Horn admits, though, "We have had financial losses each of the last few years." He refused to go into specifics.

"We have to make modifications," Horn says, "we've had a reduction in programs, a reduction of exhibits but no reduction in staff. We do have to look at how we deliver our services and be as efficient as possible."

As a PR guy, Horn puts on the rose-colored glasses, "We'd like to think it's not going to go any lower, that this is the bottom of the barrel. We're hopeful that life in 2014 will look more like it was in the first part of the 21st Century than it has for the past four of five years."

The merchants who live off The Hall's visitors sure hope he's right. Forty-eight year old Kim manages a store that sells and custom-engraves wooden baseball bats. "This is one of three jobs I have," she says, "I'm also a court clerk and a short-order cook. Because of the recession I had to do anything I could because I wanted to stay here in Otsego County."

She raises an important point; outside of Cooperstown, Otsego County (pop. 62,000) has a median income that is more than $12,000 below that of the rest of the state. Cooperstown (Pop. just fewer than 2,000) fares better with a median income $5,000 below that of the state.

Seventy-one year Dave helps run his great-nephew's souvenir shop on Main Street. "The shop's done okay during the recession but it's also changed. We used to sell 75 percent souvenirs and memorabilia and 25 percent clothes. Now, it's flipped in the last five or six years; people don't want to spend on things they can't really use. Because of that switch to more clothing we've been able to at least maintain rather than lose sales."

Sixty-eight year old Pat is also helping family. She helps out at her daughter's non-baseball-related boutique that sells children's toys, games and clothing. "It's been troublesome," she tells me referring to the recession, "more than troublesome."

"I would say we are down at least 20-to-25 percent and that's no small thing for a small business."

Pat says online shopping compounds the problem. "It's difficult for a 'brick-and-mortar' store to generate loyalty and with tourism down that only makes it worse. I work here so my daughter doesn't have to pay someone to do it."

Several other stores along Main St. have similar stories; all of them saying their business has dropped anywhere from 20-to-30 percent.

Not Sure Who's Happier Here, Me or Trooper

How could I talk to someone from the Baseball Hall of Fame and *not* ask some baseball questions?

L: What impact has baseball's steroids controversy had on the HOF?

Brad Horn: We see it as a period where it has affected the way fans celebrate heroes and moments. We don't know what the long-term impact will be but we do know that certain records and milestones over the past decade are under a cloud. Fans have a disdain for steroid users. I'd say five-to-ten percent of our attendance drop could be attributed to that. But we can't ignore it. We do refer to it in our 'Today's Game' section; it is a part of the game's history."

L: Will there come a time when the steroid users will be admitted to The Hall?

H: Only time will tell. We have a process, more than 75-years old, by which players are elected to The Hall, the voting by the Baseball Writers Association of America. And, we have specific criteria for election that include character, sportsmanship and integrity. The writers have not seen fit to give any player associated with, or suspected of association with steroids more than 50 percent of the vote (election requires mention on 75 percent of the ballots).

L: I saw Pete Rose's uniform in The Hall. If you have his uniform, why not have Pete (banned from Major League Baseball for life for gambling on his own team's games)?

Pete Rose May Not Be in the HOF But His Uniform Is!

H: You cannot tell the story of baseball history and *not* mention the all-time hits leader but our rules state that anyone banned by Major League Baseball is not eligible for induction into The Hall.

L: Let me play devil's advocate. What about Ty Cobb? Amongst other things, he was a racist and an all around sonuvabitch.

H: We set the rules for selection and frankly the selection process is reflective of the times. Cobb was elected in the first class in 1936. Obviously for that era, his crimes were not egregious enough to not be honored in this institution.

Chapter 12 – Fredonia.2

Friday August 30 – Cooperstown, NY-Fredonia, NY

I wish I could stay in Cooperstown longer. My half-day at the Baseball Hall of Fame was merely a tease but there's more to this place than just the HOF. First of all, it is simply a beautiful village in a magical forest setting.

The people in this tourist town are very friendly and it seems more sincere than a plastic "buy my stuff" kind of friendly. Then there is the history. Judge William Cooper founded the village in 1786. His sixth child, James Fenimore Cooper, is generally considered America's first great novelist. He is best known for the classic *Last of the Mohicans*. Finally, there is the Stagecoach Coffee House and Roastery (31 Pioneer Street, Cooperstown, N.Y. 13326, 607-547-6229). A small, family-run business, it is by far the best locally owned coffee house I've visited in more than 6,000 miles – great, freshly roasted coffee, good food and friendly service.

Alas, I must leave to focus on my primary mission and so I hit the road for my next stop, Fredonia, NY. Before leaving Cooperstown, however, I drop a resume off at the Hall of Fame. What the hell, one can always dream.

My tight budget changes my itinerary; I really can't afford to meander on U.S. Routes, state and county roads as much as I did on the eastward leg and so I will be driving more Interstates. For my interviews I will still stick to the small towns and cities off that heavily beaten path whenever I can. Moreover, I originally planned to take a southern route home; the economies and the cultures are so different. Now, I must drive straight and true across the top of America. Still, I will visit at least 16 states and interview hundreds of people before I am finished.

I take N.Y. Route 28 back to I-90/NY State Thruway. Knowing a 200 mile high speed, scenery blurring drive lies ahead, I savor the rolling, twisting route through mostly farmland and the occasional small town. On the bright side, there are service areas on the thruway every 40-miles or so, each with restrooms for my 66-year old prostate, its own 24-hour Starbucks and a convenient patch of grass for Trooper's micro-bladder.

Aside from its geographic convenience I choose Fredonia, NY with half a mind to compare it to Fredonia, KS. In truth, there is no comparison beyond the name. While both Fredonia's are in the heart of farm country, it ends there. Driving into this village I immediately feel the energy of a place that might not be thriving post-recession but is certainly alive and well. The New York version is not only near I-90 and several other main highways it is also home to the State University of New York's Fredonia campus and its 5,500 students. Fredonia, KS is off the main transportation routes and is dying off the vine.

Lake Erie State Park at Sunset

As an added bonus, my campground in Lake Erie State Park is right on the southern shore of that Great Lake. The downside is that this state park is not nearly as remote or quiet as my "home" near Cooperstown. The campground is large and jammed with land yachts this Labor Day Weekend. They are packed in like sardines and my tiny tent is dwarfed between two of the behemoths.

Saturday August 31 – Fredonia, NY

New York State has what I think is a unique jurisdictional system. Each county is basically divided into towns and cities, except New York City, which swallows up five counties or boroughs. The towns in this case can be very large and made up of several incorporated villages. Such is the case with Fredonia in rural Chautauqua County. It has a population of 11,400 according to the 2011 Census. Fredonia, NY would hardly be considered a "village" in other parts of the country.

Here is an interesting historical side note. According to Wikipedia:

"In 1821, William Hart dug the first well specifically to produce natural gas in the United States in the Village of Fredonia on the banks of Canadaway Creek in Chautauqua County, New York. It was 27 feet deep, excavated with shovels by hand, and its gas pipeline was hollowed out logs sealed with tar and rags. It supplied enough natural gas for lights in two stores, two shops and a grist mill (currently the village's Fire Station) by 1825. Expanding on Hart's work, the Fredonia Gas Light Company was eventually formed in 1858, becoming the first American natural gas company. The site of the first gas well is marked by a stone monument in downtown Fredonia."

And, now I also know why there are so many Fredonia's around America:

"The Village of Fredonia was incorporated in 1829. The original name for the area was Canadaway (from the Indian word *Ganadawao*, meaning *among the hemlocks*). Senator Samuel Latham Mitchill coined the name 'Fredonia" by coupling the English word "freedom" with a Latin ending. He proposed it as a replacement name for the United States. He obviously failed in that regard, but it became the name of many towns and cities."

Barker's Common – Fredonia, NY

Saturday morning is Farmer's Market time on a blocked off street just beyond Barker's Commons, Fredonia's large village green. Complete with an old freshly painted white gazebo at one end and a large fountain at its center, The Commons two-square blocks of grass are shaded by large, ancient oaks and hemlocks with many benches set within for quiet contemplation. No contemplating here, I want to talk to a farmer about the area's agriculture. I know New York's Finger Lakes Region north of Corning in the middle of the state is Wine Country but I've seen many vineyards in this area and I am curious; Fredonia is 170 miles from Corning.

I find my perfect source. He is a tall white-haired man in the first farmer's market stall I see. Sixty-eight year old Richard Feinen is the third generation to farm his family's land two miles outside of Fredonia. I quickly learn that the Concord Grape is The King here.

Welch's (Concord) Grape Juice Starts Here

"Western New York is where the fruit juice business started," he explains. "Grapes want to ferment and it's hard to stop it. In 1869 Dr. Thomas Welch (from nearby Watertown, NY) invented a pasteurization process to prevent grapes from fermenting. He did it for religious purposes; many people did not want to drink wine for communion."

By the way, if that last name sounds familiar, you're right; Dr. Welch, along with son Charles, ultimately founded the Welch's Grape Juice Company in 1890. Today, Western New York grows 68% of the state's total processing grape crop. It is by far the largest legal cash crop in Chautauqua County.

As for the recession, Feinen says it helped him in a way. "More and more people want to buy local,; they want to know what they're eating. In part it's because of the recession but folks also want to know where their food is coming from what with salmonella in melons and the like." Feinen says local markets and a produce stand at his farm kept things stable during the recession.

Manufacturing has drifted away from this area over the past few decades and it shows in the data; educational services, tourist accommodations and food services provide nearly 40 percent of the employment in Fredonia. The Great recession still found its targets here. As in many small towns across America, empty storefronts populate the downtown streets.

Twenty-five year old Jeffrey LeTrey works part time at the Cortland Extension Service in nearby Portland, NY. They do research on the management of grape production. Ironically, he earned his degree in Environmental Science at the University of Oregon, south of another Portland.

As a University of Washington Husky fan, I will spare you my hatred for the Oregon Ducks other than to say, "What kind of nickname is that for sports teams, The Ducks?" LeTrey has no answer. As usual, I digress.

LeTrey moved back here in 2011 and it took him almost a year to find his part time, low paying job, and the major consequence is that he had to move back in with his folks. Can you say Boomerang Generation?

Forty five year old Brian Davis describes himself as a stay at home dad. He used to own a combined small café, arts and crafts store in Fredonia. Timing as they say, is everything; he opened his business in 2007, right before the recession became "official."

Luckily his 44-year old wife, Adrian McCormick, is a tenured professor at SUNY Fredonia. While Adrian's position saved the couple, the recession still crept its way into their lives. "We used a quarter of my pension, $25,000, as collateral for loans to finance the start Brian's business."

"We started off okay," says Brian, "but as the recession deepened, it slowly killed the business. We had to really tighten our belts and restructure everything"

Adrian adds, "Even after the business closed the loans didn't go away. On top of that we still had student loan debt sitting out there. It got pretty ugly. For a year or two we were just paying minimums and for a while we couldn't pay at all on one of the business loans. Now, we'll owe on it until I retire."

"I'm still going through it," Brian says. "I learned all my business skills and techniques in a different pre-recession world. Everything is different – things like funding and revenue, how you structure it, the risks you're willing to take. I have to relearn everything."

Thirty-one year old Erin is a "domestic engineer," running the family finances and caring for her two children. Her husband works for a non-profit community development and housing service. "When the recession hit," she says, "he was working on his Masters Degree. It took him more than a year to find a job. We were living in Massachusetts but had to move here when my husband found his job. Things got very tight for a while and we had to dip into our savings. Luckily we had some savings left when he found work."

I wonder to myself, "How many American lives did The Great Recession change forever?"

Chapter 13 – A Small taste of Michigan

Monday September 2 – Fredonia, NY-Meronci, MI

For the first time in my journey, I have nothing to say about my drive from one location to another. With a few exceptions, such is freeway driving in the United States. Instead, I settle in to listen to an eBook, *Infamous,* a novel by Ace Atkins. It is a wry, gritty crime drama set in the 1930s featuring George "Machine Gun" Kelly. I am enthralled as the time and the miles fly by.

I actually didn't know I was going to Meronci, MI. In fact, it doesn't even appear on Google Maps unless you search for it – which I didn't. It seems there isn't much in Southern Michigan, except for Toledo, OH. Look at a map.

When choosing a destination I look for a place within about 300 miles of my current location with nearby camping. My preference is a city, county, state or national park/recreation area, etc. The problem in Southern Michigan, at least according to Google Maps, is that the nearest campground to any town or city – other than Toledo – is about 45 miles away. I look beyond my normal driving distance and find the Lake Hudson State Recreation Area, about 20 miles from the City of Adrian, MI. It is well over 300 miles from Fredonia, NY and a five-hour drive, all freeways. I am resigned.

My Only "Neighbor" in the Lake Hudson Campground

To my surprise and relief, the little town of Meronci is only eight miles from the campground. Even better, on this Labor Day Monday, everyone is leaving camp. When I awake in the morning my only neighbor is a little yellow and black bird observing me from a nearby tree. Otherwise I have the campground to myself and, just for the hell of it, I throw off my clothing and romp buck-naked for a while. What a great feeling! Trooper looks embarrassed. The bird could care less.

Tuesday September 3 – Meronci, MI

Meronci is barely in Michigan. Its southern border is the Ohio State Line. Downtown is just three blocks long. There is one gas station, a traffic light, a small locally owned grocery store, and two, count 'em, two pizza parlors. On this Tuesday the streets are all but empty.

Founded in 1838, Morenci and environs is primarily agricultural, mostly corn. Palm Plastics was a large (for this area) manufacturing plant here but, thanks to the recession, closed down late last year throwing more than 200 people out of work. Forty-nine year old Bill Foster was the maintenance man in that factory. "I saw the handwriting on the wall and got out early. It had a ripple affect throughout the town here."

Ripple affect, indeed. In 2011 the median income in Morenci was about $35,000, more than $10,000 below the state median. Home sales dropped from just under 40 in 2011 to about 20 in 2012. There were just two new home building permits in 2012.

In a way, Bill Foster was lucky; he immediately found work with a former employer and now drives RVs and construction trailers all over the country and into Canada delivering them to customers. But, while the salary is the same as it was at Palm Plastics, it really isn't.

"My job is now in Indiana and I have to drive 80 miles to get there," he says, "but at least I'm working. The problem is, I'm away from home a lot more."

Ironically, the recession drove him out of this job in the first place. "After Hurricane Katrina and then with the recession, sales of these trailers went way down, a lot of manufacturers closed and so I left for the job at Palm. Funny how things work out."

Fifty-seven year old William Rezoski has held the same job for thirty-five years but the recession still wormed its way into his life.

"I'm a machinist at a factory in Fayette, OH (just south of the state line from Morenci). We make parts for Ford Trucks. Truck sales suffered during the recession and we cut way back; we lost more than a hundred people, more than half the workforce. My job wasn't threatened per se, but my hours got cut way back. Where I was once making tons of overtime, I was lucky if I got 40 hours a week. We had to cut way back at home."

Sixty-five year old Pearl Phelps owns one of the two pizza places in town, Pearl's Pizza Palace. She says she saw business drop off a bit since last year, "but not as badly as some of the other businesses in town. I don't know why." She says she is starting to see things bounce back "just a bit."

I find it most interesting that the owner of the largest farm in the area, State Line Farms, declines an interview. That's happened maybe six or seven times in almost 7,000 miles.

As I've noted before, many large family-owned farms across the country pretty much held their own, if not prospered, during the recession. As I drive by State Line Farms on my way to camp, I slow to see what I can see. Besides the very large twin grain silos, the big yard next to the barn is filled with what appears to be several brand new shiny tractors and other equipment.

Perhaps the owner declined to speak with me because he feels the embarrassment of riches. This is only speculation on my part. Let's call it an educated guess.

After my short stay in Morenci I will briefly re-visit the state of Illinois.

Chapter 14 – Life on the Mississippi

Oglesby, IL is merely a one night stand, or sleepover. I've already passed through – and written about – The Land of Lincoln and I do not want to duplicate states unless there are compelling reasons to do so.

Driving away from Oglesby I enjoy about 40 miles of county and state roads before getting on bustling, high-speed U.S. 20 West. Economically, the area is still agricultural, mostly corn as usual. As we edge into September the corn is turning brown and many farmers are cutting the stalks almost to the ground, the remnant chips blowing like tan snow across the roads.

I am in the Illinois River Valley and this is a much different Illinois scenically than other parts of the state I've seen. The valley is thick with lush forests dotted only by the occasional farm, unlike the rest of Illinois where it is flat with cornfield after cornfield, interrupted by the occasional cornfield.

As the miles speed by, I'm suddenly struck by a thought, "Wow, I am actually on the last leg of this great journey." The thought arouses mixed feelings. On the one hand, this is the trip of a lifetime, one that not many can experience in the manner I have. I've learned a lot about America and Americans and I've learned a bit about myself.

I love being on the road. I love visiting new places, meeting and talking to new people and soaking in the forever changing scenery of America. I love learning about the history of this great land, especially the local histories that did not make my mostly ignored school texts. The flip side is, I like showering every day and I like doing so without sharing my shower with thousands of dead bugs. I know I will like lying down every night in the same bed, a real bed. Life is a series of tradeoffs or, as Billy Joel sang in "Say Good-Bye to Hollywood," life is a series of hellos and good-byes.

My realization that I am almost done brings another revelation. I started out with the idea that I will gather the stories of people and how The Great Recession affected their lives. I made a conscious decision to concentrate mostly on the smaller cities and towns, what I call The Real America. While I've accomplished that goal, I realize I've also collected the story of small-town America itself and, I don't think it is a commonly known story. While I will elaborate in my final chapter, regardless of what we hear from Washington, D.C., there is no sweeping recovery. In many parts of The Real

America, the recession is still all too real and very present.

On my eastbound drive, you may recall, I was forced to miss a planned "ceremonial" crossing and stopping at the Mississippi River. The Missouri Monsoon still sloshes around in my memory. Heading west I've chosen for my crossing the small city of Keokuk, Iowa. My preliminary research shows it to be a very interesting place indeed.

As I drive into Keokuk on U.S. 61/Main Street I am immediately struck by the large number of empty, closed down stores, many more than in most any other place I've visited. What makes it more curious is the fact that Keokuk does not otherwise look like a city in its death throes. Note to self, find out the reason for this dichotomy.

In the meantime, Ron, who runs the Hickory Haven Campground where I will domicile for the next two nights, tells me that the Iowa (Mississippi) river towns depend much less upon farming than the rest of the state. Historically, their economic driver was manufacturing. Sadly, that is truly history now; over the years – beginning before the recession – the companies either consolidated and/or simply moved the jobs, many of them overseas. The local bitterness is still palpable.

But Keokuk retains one very large manufacturer, French multi-national Roquette. According to Roquette's Website, "It transforms renewable resources corn, wheat, potatoes and peas - into an extensive line of high quality ingredients for a wide range of food and non-food industries throughout the world." Roquette is a major producer of starch and the sweetener Sorbitol.

Roquette Plant – Keokuk, IA

The company has offices, manufacturing plants and agents worldwide to the tune of €2.5 Billion in annual revenue. Depending upon which Website you visit, the company employs anywhere from 2,000-5,000 people at its huge plant here in the Keokuk-Lee County area. The Website is mum on the subject. Bottom line, Roquette is key to Keokuk's economic future.

Friday September 7 – Keokuk, Iowa

Keokuk began in 1820 as a trading post along the Mississippi River. The city is named for Keokuk (1767–1848), Chief of the Sauk Tribe and a long time ally of the United States. In 1827 John Jacob Astor opened a branch of his American Fur Company here. It was the boyhood home of the late billionaire Howard Hughes. The town's history, however, is really tied to The Civil War.

In addition to its participation in the Underground Railroad that helped runaway slaves to freedom in the North, Keokuk was also a key supply and debarkation point for Union Forces headed to the war's southern battles. The Union set up hospitals here for the returning wounded and those hospitals remained after the war to become a key part of the area's economy. Confederate forces retreating from the south came through – and the wounded cared for in Keokuk. There is a national cemetery in Keokuk with the remains of both Union and Confederate soldiers.

Stark Antebellum Contrasts Along the Mississippi River – Keokuk, IA

I see more of the history as I drive along the river and see the classic antebellum mansions, many of them in pristine condition. Some of them are not; there are a few old and abandoned big houses along the river as well.

One of its leading citizens hopes Keokuk's history can be a big part of the city's economic future. William "Bill" Logan is the fourth generation Chief Executive Officer of his family's business, The State Central Bank. Sitting nearby is Bill's son Tyler, the fifth generation and current bank president.

The bank's magnificent five-floor 75-year old building is still one of the tallest in town. Logan's commitment to Keokuk's history is right there for all to see. Spanning one entire wall of the main banking area on the first floor are five intricate, colorful murals depicting Keokuk's past, present and future.

Not Many Bank Interiors Look Like the Beautiful Main Floor of Keokuk's State Central Bank

Logan's hope that history will help build Keokuk's future is born from a steady population and subsequent business decline that began before the recent downturn. As I talk to Bill Logan about this, he explains the connection to the many empty stores along Main Street.

"Over the last 15 years our population went from 20,000 to where it's now under 10,000," he says. The U.S. Census shows the decline, while significant, is not as serious as Logan claims. In 1990 The Census showed a population of 12,491, a bit over 10,000 in 2010. Still, population decline translates to fewer customers, hence the empty stores lining Main Street.

Bill Logan says Keokuk came through the recession, in his words, the same as everyone else. "We had shorter workweeks, layoffs, people not taking haircuts. Maybe we got by a little better than most because at least some of the factories stayed in Keokuk."

The greater threat to Keokuk's economy over the last five years was a ten-month lockout at the Roquette Plant. Bill Logan says the town was even able to weather that. "They had strike benefits and they all got through okay."

Clearly Bill Logan is reluctant to paint a dim picture of his town. But when pressed he reluctantly reveals that The Great Recession really did visit upon Keokuk. "Five factories either just closed or moved," he reluctantly admits, "and that cost hundreds of jobs. We lost probably twenty downtown stores during the recession."

Keokuk is shrinking but it isn't dying thanks to the Roquette plant and another good-sized factory that makes steel casings but it is by no means a wealthy town. The median household income in 2011 was only $34,653, almost $15,000 below that of the entire state.

Perhaps most telling about Keokuk's economic health are the unemployment and new home construction figures. Since 2009 unemployment has hovered around 10 percent. In 2008 there were 11 permits issued for new home construction. In the ensuing years a total of ten have been issued.

Once again the national news out of our nation's capital is at odds with reality. While the politicos announced the recession as "official" at the end of 2007, it didn't hit many small cities and towns until one-to-three years later and, as I discover again here in Keokuk, many small towns and cities in The Real America are still suffering.

Yet another digression; later in the day, I'm standing in line at the only Starbucks in Keokuk, located inside of a Target. I see a young woman in her 20s wearing a black T-shirt with a bejeweled fist on the front displaying a raised middle finger. I love it!

"Is that your commentary on the world?" I ask.

Without a beat she replies. "It is today." I love it!

A few moments later, as I'm walking to the Jeep, I see the same young woman standing by an older white Camaro hardtop, shopping cart at her side. She is obviously upset as she fumbles through her large purse, apparently looking for her keys. Then, she looks through the driver's side window and bursts into tears.

In my world, chivalry is not dead. I walk over. "Looks like your world just got worse," I opine.

"Sniff. Sniff. I locked my keys in the car and I can't reach my husband."

"I have some experience with this," I tell her. After checking around the driver's window to see if I can move it, I go back to the Jeep and return with everyman's tool for locked-in car keys, the handy dandy wire hanger.

After further assessing the situation I'm thinking it should be a snap; I've done it so many times for myself. Carefully pushing the window inward to create enough space, I bend the now unwound hangar, bent sharply at the end to grab the lock button and start feeding it through the small opening.

With rising confidence and the satisfied feeling of a Good Samaritan I easily position the hangar's end right where I want it and snap it back to pull the lock upward. The hangar slips away, the lock unopened. No problem; in all the years I've done this, I've never succeeded on the first try. Thirty minutes later, I'm still trying and in the 90-degree heat I am sweating profusely. The young woman, still leaking an occasional tear, patiently stands by holding Trooper on his leash (can't leave my buddy in the sweltering Jeep). By now I realize I need some help; I can't maintain pressure on the window with one hand and with the other get enough torque on the hanger to pop the button. I see a young man exit his car a few slots down and start walking for the store. "Hey," I yell. "Have ya ever boosted a car?"

I am only half serious but the dude smiles and says, "Sure. Be right there."

He goes back to his car and returns with a screwdriver, which he promptly inserts and angles at the top of the window giving me a lot more room and two hands with which to work.

After several more futile – but closer – tries, I notice the woman is starting to cry again. "Hmmm," I say to myself. "Maybe I should try to take her mind off things."

Looking over I see a small firm tummy bulge just above her belt and immediately blunder into the land no man should ever enter. But, the bulge is so firm I'm almost convinced. "Looks like you're expecting," I say.

Without hesitating, she answers, "Nope."

DOH!!! I immediately redden, turn my head away and return to my task.

Luckily, at that very moment, the hanger's hook catches on the lock and this time it pops open. Thank Gawd!!!

Not knowing how to respond to her profuse thanks – I am still embarrassed – I immediately withdraw.

Hey, at least I took her mind off things.

Saturday September 7 – Keokuk, Iowa-Caledonia, Minnesota

With the exception of some high speed U.S. Highway driving today, I will be mostly on county and state roads running parallel to, but several miles away from, the Mississippi River. This is still Iowa and, except for the occasional "corn fed" beef on the hoof, it is again cornfield after cornfield, interrupted by the occasional cornfield. I still prefer it to freeway/interstate driving. As I near the Minnesota State Line the straight roads and cornfields begin to give way to more S-curves, hills, thick stands of trees and then forest. The occasional farm always a presence as well.

Sunday September 8 – Caledonia, Minnesota-La Crosse, Wisconsin

My plan for today doesn't include a trip back across the Mississippi River to La Crosse, WI but as I survey downtown Caledonia, MN this morning it dawns on me that I've seen and written about too many Caledonia's; towns with populations of 1,500-2,500. Farms surround them, many of which are doing well while the downtowns are deathly quiet with For Rent signs in empty stores all along their main Streets. La Crosse here I come.

In this neck of the woods La Crosse is THE big city with a 2012 population of 51,647. It has a long history, beginning with French fur traders who traveled the Mississippi in the late 17th Century. There is no formal written record of any visits to the area until Zebulon Pike – yes, *that* Pike – explored this part of the Mississippi under the American Flag in 1805. Pike wouldn't reach his Peak until 1806.

And, guess what! According to the Wisconsin Historical Society, Pike actually named the location for a game he noticed the natives playing. The sticks with which they were catching and tossing a small ball resembled a bishop's crozier or, in French, a La Crosse. The first White settlement here in 1841 was a fur trading post. La Crosse became a city in 1856. The city's thriving Historic Downtown began to grow from that point in time.

Much of Downtown La Crosse Looks Like This

My research shows La Crosse is one of those places that weathered The Great Recession better than most. One reason is the fact that the two largest employers are the Gundersen Lutheran Medical Center and The Mayo Clinic Health System. The city also is home to three regional colleges and universities. Several major corporations have their international headquarters here as well, including:

- Trane, the air conditioning company now owned by Ingersoll Rand
- City Brewing Co., formally Heileman.
- Kwik Trip, regional gas and convenience stores (believe me, they are all over the midwest)
- Logistics Health, Inc., "Health care solutions for government and commercial customers."

Other indicators also show La Crosse's endurance. Home sales remain steady, running mostly between 600-700 over the past five years although new home construction permits are half of their peak 49 in 2004.

In 2010 the Wisconsin Council on Children and Families studied the recession's impact on La Crosse County. While unemployment was up, it was still nearly 4 percent below the national average. The loss of jobs, ironically, meant a loss of health insurance in this health-care-centric city. Still, I hear some intriguing stories as I enjoy a latte sitting outside of a small downtown espresso house (Only one Starbuck's shows up in my La Crosse search!). The most interesting tales come from two young sisters headed for lunch at a nearby restaurant. They look like students and, while there are some stories worth telling in this age group, there are also so many who hardly have a clue about the recession or its affects.

Twenty-two year old Kelsey is a recent college grad who holds a part time job running an after school child care program. "It took probably more than a year of relentless searching before I could find this job," she tells me.

Kelsey's employer is a non-profit organization and, while she runs an after-school program, the organization runs a day school and relies primarily on federal grants for its funding. "The day school education programs we can offer are diminished. The purse strings are tighter, cuts in staff, cuts in programs and cuts in benefits," says Kelsey.

"Luckily I don't need many of those benefits right now because I'm young enough where I can still mooch off my parents insurance and, my husband recently left the military and he still has some benefits."

"Still," she continues, "my husband is a full time student now and we are living pay check to pay check. It's rough."

"Do you have any kids?" I ask.

As she begins to answer, Kelsey looks up as if the realization just strikes her. "No," she starts slowly, "and I probably couldn't afford it if I wanted to."

Younger sister Brook displays a savvy maturity that belies her 19-years. "I'm still a full-time student," she says, "and I am working as a server in a restaurant to pay my entire way through. I even worked my way through high school."

"So," I observe, "the recession began while you were in high school; probably didn't affect you."

Brook spears me with laser eyes as if I just fell off the turnip truck, "Are you kidding? It was almost impossible to find a job. People much older who were losing their higher paying jobs were going down to take the jobs that high school kids would normally take."

"I didn't work my entire freshman year because I couldn't find a job. I had to use my own savings to pay for school. I'm lucky; most students paying their way through school didn't have savings. I spent probably $5,000 a semester."

This determined young woman reminds me of something I'm seeing all around the country; we are strong and resilient. As The Great Recession continues to blow through The Real America, we will bend in the wind but we will not break.

Chapter 15 – Me Llamo Worthington, MN

Monday September 9 – Caledonia, Minnesota-Worthington, Minnesota

As I break camp this morning it is cloudy and cool, the temperature is in the 60s. I am surprised then when I walk into Elsie's Bar and Grill, my Caledonia headquarters, and hear people talking about a forecast of record breaking temps around 100°.

There are Elsie's kinds of places in almost every small town I've visited, even the dying towns. It's the place where the ol' boys go for a sunrise breakfast, hot coffee and to talk about the weather, tractors and hog prices. You can get two over medium, bacon, hash browns and coffee for $3.95, biscuits and gravy $4.95.

If you're in a hurry, you can sit at the counter. The skinny bleached blonde waitress in jeans way too tight for her age, a face heavily made-up to hide the hard lifelines and a cigarette raspy voice will take your order and call you honey. The bar is in the back and later in the morning the older ol' boys will filter in and start playing poker. I love Elsie's! By the time I leave after eating and writing an hour and a half later the sun is blazing and I know the forecast is correct.

I'll have to travel almost 150 miles on I-90 west today to Worthington at the other end of the state but first I'll enjoy about 80 miles on mostly county and state roads. I am surprised at the condition of Minnesota's state highways; they are in terrible disrepair, by far the worst I've seen. There are cracks and bumps in the surfaces, providing a jarring ride I usually experience on the county roads. More surprising, I see little or no roadwork along the way.

These roads are twisty and rolling with plenty of farmland still around me. After awhile, the road straightens and the land flattens. The crops are mostly corn and soybean in fact; I'm seeing some of the largest cornfields ever. I am also seeing more wind farms than I've seen any place else. At one point these giant windmills on either side of the road stand as far as the eye can see. The wind power production industry has definitely taken hold across America. Am I the only one just realizing that?

I stop for gas on the outskirts of Worthington and I'm struck by a sign in the convenience store window, "Welcome to Worthington, MN, Turkey Capital (sic) of the World!" Being the wiseass that I am, even to myself, I wonder, "Are they talking about birds or people?"

Tuesday September 10 – Worthington, MN

This is the second time on my journey I am staying in a city park campground and, again, it is a delight. The rate is great – $18.00 a night – and the location fabulous. Not only is it convenient to downtown, the park, as well as the city, sits on Lake Okabena. It is a small natural lake, one-point-two square miles, located entirely within the city.

Camping on Lake Okabena

Lake Okabena and the surrounding area were first mapped in 1841 by

French explorer Joseph Nicollet. He dubbed the area Sisseton Country in honor of the local tribe of the Dakota Sioux. He named the lake using the Sioux word for "home of the heron." The City of Worthington would be incorporated about 30-years later and has a curious history. Take the town's name for example.

Many locations are named for heroes, military leaders, royalty, founders, explorers, local native tribes and chiefs; Washington, Lafayette, New York, Pennsylvania, Pikes Peak, Seattle and Georgia, for example. One of Worthington's founders went an entirely different direction; he took for the town's designation his mother-in-law's maiden name. Go figure.

From the beginning Worthington was a railroad town. It was originally called The Okabena Railway Station because that was the locale's original purpose, to serve as a way station between the two termini of the St. Paul & Sioux City Railway. That same year, 1871, Professor Ransom Humiston of Cleveland and Toledo Blade editor Dr. A.P. Miller formed a company to locate a colony of settlers along the new rail line. They chose the Okabena Station as their location and it was Dr. Miller who changed the name to honor his M-I-L. The rail yards in Worthington are still active today.

I learned of another, more curious piece of local – and more recent – history after I arrived in town. The second thing I noticed after the Turkey Capital of the World sign was the number of bodega's (three) and Mexican restaurants (two) along the three or four blocks of Worthington's main drag. This is a town of about 13,000 people and that seems like a lot of Hispanic commerce. So I am mildly shocked to learn that a little more than a third of Worthington's population *is* Hispanic.

The Hispanic Presence is Everywhere in Worthington

That's not a very big number if you compare it to cities like Laredo, TX where more than 90 percent of the people are Hispanic. Laredo is on the Mexican border; THIS is Minnesota, on the Canadian border. Curious.

The answer is economics, pure economics – and pigs not turkeys. In the mid-1980s a farm crisis nearly killed Worthington and the population began to rapidly decline. There were only about 100 Hispanics here in the mid 80s. At the same time, the town's largest employer, a pork processing plant changed hands (today it is owned by Swift). The new owners added a shift and dramatically cut wages. As word of this spread, hundreds of lower income minorities began to arrive, primarily Hispanics. Today, more than 2,000 people work at the plant.

It's been a mixed blessing for Worthington. On the one hand, JBS Swift & Co[1], the plant's official name, helped shield the area from the worst of The Great Recession. Worthington's unemployment rate "peaked" at five-point-five percent in 2010-11 and sits somewhere in the fours now. But the immigrant inflow brought the attendant problems that come along with such a dramatic demographic shift.

---

[1] In 2006, the Worthington plant was one of several Swift facilities around the country raided by the U.S. Immigration and Naturalization Service for employing undocumented immigrants. More than 200 illegal workers were arrested in Worthington.

Ryan McGaughy is Managing Editor for the Worthington Daily Globe. He's been with the newspaper for 12 years, first as a sports reporter, moving over to the news side and eventually to the Big Desk in 2006. He says the inflow of immigrants initially caused the predictable division within the town between those who thought it would ruin the city and those who saw it as a positive thing. There's a little bit of truth on both sides.

"You might notice there's a lot of construction going on," he tells me. We built a new hospital, a brand new event center and a new supermarket. But our biggest challenge as a community is housing. Many of the lower wage workers are buying the older homes and they have multiple occupants because there just isn't enough housing stock for them."

"It's going to take a major combined effort to address the challenge. You have the city and the county – even the state has gotten involved to an extent. JBS is also at the table because they realize their people need housing. It will take that kind of joint effort because Joe Schmoe local developer isn't going to go investing in housing here."

I then turned to McGaughy's personal story. He is, after all, in an industry that was all but dying before the recession began. "I don't want to say we're closing our doors; we're certainly not," he explains, "but ad revenue has been harder to come by, that's for sure and it accelerated during the recession."

"Do you fear for your job?" I ask.

"I don't think my job is threatened, per se but I do fear that one day I'll come in and someone will tell me they're going to centralize and say, for example, do the layout for the paper in Fargo where our company headquarters is located."

Finally, I can't help myself and ask McCaughy, "So, why are you the turkey capitol and not the pig capitol of the world?"

He laughs, "Oh that's from the 20s and 30s when we had a real turkey industry. Today there isn't a turkey plant in Worthington."

But, the town does celebrate its turkey heritage every September with Turkey Days, complete with turkey races. The participating turkeys are ringers, though; they have to be imported for the event.

Afternote: You might be asking yourself, "Why didn't he interview any of the Hispanics in Worthington." Lord knows I tried.

I walked into one of the restaurants, one of the bodegas and stopped several folks on the street. Nada.

Inside One of Worthington's Bodegas

Maybe they didn't trust a scruffy gringo in a straw fedora or maybe, just maybe, they are still gun shy after the 2006 raid.

Scruffy Gringo in a Straw Fedora

Chapter 16 – This Midwest is Really The Old West

Wednesday September 11 – Worthington, Minnesota-Pierre South Dakota

My next destination is Pierre (Peer), the capitol of South Dakota. It is a long haul, 240 miles on I-90 and another 30 on a two-lane highway but there aren't many decent-sized cities in North Dakota (state pop. 833,354 in 2012) and there is good camping nearby. I also like to visit state capitols; I still haven't given up on interviewing a governor or two.

While the U.S. Census considers The Dakotas part of the Midwest, the rest of us – even the Dakotans – think of them as part of The Old West. The billboards along the way confirm that. In fact, I've never seen so many billboards. For miles on end there is one nearly every hundred yards and most of them tout some tourist attraction, souvenir shop or hotel with a Western theme. There are farms sprinkled along the way but they are few and far between; I rarely see a barn or house but the hay is rolled and piled, ready to be hauled away.

Wherever I see an American flag today it is flying at half-staff in memory of those who lost their lives on that tragic 9/11/2001. It is my generation's Pearl Harbor; we will never forget where we were when we first heard of the attacks.

Then, all of a sudden, appearing out of nowhere I am in baseball player heaven, acre after acre, and row after row of tall sunflowers. I can almost see the shells being spit out in dugouts from Little League to the Majors.

At last I leave I-90 about 30 miles south of my destination and there is nothing but wide-open prairie all around. I pass through the smaller town of Ft. Pierre and cross the Missouri River to enter Pierre, which is a mild geographic surprise. I did not know the Missouri flowed through here.

Trooper Playing in the Missouri River

The river is not the only thing that separates the two towns. Pierre is in the Central Time Zone while Ft. Pierre is Mountain Time. If you commute to work from Ft. Pierre to Pierre you have to get up an hour earlier. That's a long commute.

Thursday September 12 – Pierre, SD-Rapid City, SD

Thirty-five percent of the work force in Pierre is either city, state or federal government so I'm guessing while there may have been some cuts, Pierre didn't suffer during the recession as much as other cities.

It is early morning and I am breakfasting in Pier 347, home to the city's only operating espresso machine and free Wi Fi. Sitting at the table next to me is a small group and one man starts talking about legislative sessions. My ears perk up. He is a tall, distinguished looking white-haired gentleman and as he stands to leave I ask, "Excuse me sir, are you a member of the legislature?"

"No," he replies, "but I direct the legislative staff. I'm Jim" That's good enough for me. I explain my project and he is a fount of helpful information.

"The legislature meets only in the winter," he explains, "so there aren't many of us around."

"What about the governor?" I ask hopefully.

"He might be around. We are probably the most open state government in the country. Just walk on in to his office and ask to see Stacy, his scheduler. If he's there she can probably get you in for a few minutes." Colorado Governor Hickenlooper can learn from these people.

Buoyed by this news I finish my espresso and head straight for South Dakota's magnificent state capitol building (Aren't they all?).

South Dakota State Capitol

Inside, the capitol building, with all its marble, gilded ceilings and shiny wooden trim, it's like a giant mausoleum; there is nobody in the lobby or under the rotunda, not even a State Trooper. I find the governor's office and two receptionists with warm smiling faces greet me. There is no formal, authoritarian self-importance here. After explaining my mission, one of the young ladies offers, "Have a seat and I'll go get Stacy." Jim was right.

In just a minute or two a smiling Stacy comes out with sincere apologies, "I'm sorry, the governor is in D.C. through tomorrow but come with me. Let's go see if the Lt. Governor is in." Just like that. Unfortunately, the Lt. Governor is likewise out of town but I am nonetheless impressed with the helpful friendliness of the staff. I will later find out that just about everyone else in Pierre is "not in." I spend the next 90-minutes patrolling a virtually empty downtown with nary a useful interview to be had. I make an executive decision to leave town.

Google Maps tells me Rapid City, South Dakota's second largest city (pop. 69,854 in 2012), is only 145 miles away – and, only 25 miles from Mt. Rushmore (on my Bucket List agenda!). There is plenty of camping in the area. Oh boy!

I head west on U.S. 14, across rolling hills, the broad expanse of the South Dakota prairie and many more sunflower farms. I will only have a short hop on I-90 and into Rapid City. In the meantime I am entering, oops, leaving the town of Cotton (pop. 12!).

I get on I-90 and the hills become a little bigger, their edges a little sharper. I am entering Black Hills Country. I can't explain why but I'm not really looking forward to Rapid City. Maybe it's the name, if not boring, it sounds fictitious. I will learn quickly; Rapid City is anything but boring.

Friday September 13 – Rapid City, SD

The 1874 cry of, "There's gold in them thar hills!" led indirectly to the founding of Rapid City as a White man's settlement. Of course, The Lakota Sioux inhabited the land long before Western Culture arrived. The Lakota call Rapid City "Fast Water Mni Luzahan" for nearby Rapid Creek.

The Black Hills at Sunset

A group of disappointed but entrepreneurial miners founded the city in 1876, originally calling it "Hay Camp." With its location on the eastern slopes of the hills, they marketed it as "Gateway to the Black Hills. According to Wikipedia:

"Although the Black Hills became a popular tourist destination in the late 1890s, it was a combination of local efforts, the popularity of the automobile, and construction of improved highways that brought tourists to the Black Hills in large numbers after World War I. Gutzon Borglum, already a famous sculptor, began work on Mount Rushmore in 1927 and his son, Lincoln Borglum, continued the carving of the presidents' faces in rock following his father's death in 1941. The work was halted due to pressures leading to the US entry into World War II and the massive sculpture was declared complete in 1941. Although tourism sustained the city throughout the Great Depression of the 1930s, the gasoline rationing of World War II had a devastating effect on the tourist industry in the town, but this was more than made up for by the war-related growth."

Farming, of course, was always part of the local economy. Later came Ellsworth Air Force Base and the population almost doubled. In the early 21st Century the Black Hills region was enjoying a manufacturing boom. The Great Recession un-boomed the area but did not kill it. Two major factories closed their doors during the recession and put several hundred people out of work. It more than doubled the ridiculously low unemployment rate to a little more than four percent, hence the relatively minor impact on the area. This is where I came to like and respect the people and the city, despite its contribution to the deterioration of the Sioux Nation. More on that in a moment.

Destination Rapid City, a very involved and active private downtown development group, refused to roll over. Dan Seftner is president of Destination Rapid City. He displays a can-do attitude that often leads to success. He points out other times such as when the big box stores were sucking the life out of downtowns around America. "It's no different today. If you were heavily leveraged to begin with and could not take a setback then you were in trouble. If you weren't, you could take advantage of things and make them work for you on the other side of the coin."

That is not just Seftner's theory; it is a truism taught in Economics 101 and the results are evident everywhere in downtown Rapid City. Virtually every place I've visited so far has had its share of closed and empty downtown stores. There is not one empty store here that I can see. It is a vibrant downtown. "I'd say we are at least 95 percent leased in the downtown area," says Seftner.

The mid-morning streets are spotlessly clean and crowded with locals and tourists. There are numerous cafes and restaurants with sidewalk seating, countless Western-themed shops, art galleries, native crafts stores and amazing public art, much of it privately funded. For example, there are all those presidents.

John Adams   Thomas Jefferson   James Madison

About 15-years ago a group of businessmen decided to use Rapid City's proximity to Mt. Rushmore for an ambitious project; they would seek private funding to create bronze statues of every U.S. president and place them on downtown street corners. Thus, Rapid City became the City of Presidents. The statues, either life-size or about two-thirds scale, are remarkable likenesses of our nation's leaders and the tourists love 'em. Throughout the morning I see families taking photos of themselves next to their favorites.

Now, let's talk about the Native Americans in and around Rapid City. I spoke with a local NPR news producer who told me the presidential statues initially created quite a controversy because there was nothing to honor the great Lakota Chiefs. "We are currently standing on Sioux Treaty Land," he points out. Indeed, the only thing I saw even close to honoring the Sioux was an unlabeled statue of a Lakota woman and her child. Can you say "tokenism?"

"Token" Statue for the Sioux

And, as with the Latinos of Worthington, MN, the few Native Americans I see downtown have no interest in speaking to a scruffy-looking White guy in a white Burlington Northern Santa Fe Railroad baseball cap. I'll spare you the photo.

Aside from the slights and tokenism to the Lakota, there is much to like here. For one thing, there are many Starbucks, always a factor for moi and, I just love Rapid City's downtown. In addition to the busy streets, restaurants, shops and presidents' statues there is an abundance of other public art, most of it pleasing to the eye. You can almost feel the heart of this city thumping.

And, finally, there are unique individuals to be met – to me they add color to the fabric of any vibrant city.

There's "thirty something" Susan Ricci from Wayne, New Jersey of all places, owning and operating a small downtown museum dedicated to the American Bison. Not only that, for a while she owned a bison ranch. Really?

This Italian/Jewish Jersey Girl has been in Rapid City for 16-years. "I moved out here because I wanted to work with the Native American Tribes," she says, "and I got hired by, of all things, a tribal bison preservation organization. They work with tribes all across the country to restore the herds on their land.

"They hired me to do office work but their development director quit and they just told me I was the new development director. Then, I met and fell in love with a buffalo herd manager from Montana and we had a little buffalo ranch here in South Dakota."

"Oy vey," I think to myself, "her mother must've plotzed; It's a shonda (a shame in Yiddush)!!!!"

Okay, it's one thing to meet a bison-lovin' Jersey Girl in South Dakota but how about a street cart vendor selling Nathan's Famous (of Coney Island) Hot Dogs on a street corner? There he was, a 25-year young chap joyfully pushing the tube steaks.

"This used to be a part time thing for me," says Doug Christiansen, "but I made some bad choices at my other job and they let me go so I started doing this full time. Best decision I ever made!"

I'm astounded. "How the hell did a 25-year old Rapid City boy end up selling Nathan's Hot Dogs here on a street corner?"

"I saw a guy selling 'em on a street corner and asked him if he wanted another guy selling 'em on another street corner. Now I'm the only guy selling hot dogs on a street corner. We roll this thing around during the day to different locations and we're doing great."

"But how did he come by Nathan's?" I press. "I know they've become a chain but they are usually associated with Coney Island and New York."

"I know and I've never been out of Rapid City but everyone knows Nathan's as a brand now," he sagely explains.

Ironically, when I hit the local Safeway to stock up for the next week, I see a whole section of refrigerated Nathan's Hot Dogs in the deli section. Without hesitation I buy a couple of packages.

I haven't watched TV since hitting the road and, frankly, I haven't missed it

– except for sports. The Mariners' season is long dead and so is my interest but it's now football season. I have more than casual interest in the rejuvenated University of Washington Huskies and the sky-high expectation Seattle Seahawks. I have insane interest in the Hawks game tonight (Sunday).

It's only the second game of the season and probably the biggest second game in NFL history as the Seahawks take on archrival San Francisco at home and on national TV. Not only are they bitter rivals they are two of the NFC teams favored to make it to the Super Bowl. I must see this game. I Google search Rapid City sports bars with particular emphasis on menu prices. I need a big screen and a cheap meal. Shooters, on Main Street just west of downtown looks like the place.

I'm wearing my white Mariners home jersey because I didn't bring along any Seahawks gear. How shortsighted of me. I grab a table in the bar, one of those high ones with tall stools, right in front of a double widescreen wall. I've already talked to the manager to ensure the game is on at least one of these screens. I order a large Diet Pepsi, the specialty of the house bacon cheeseburger and fries and warm up by watching the end of the Broncos-Giants game. Does life get any better?

Finally, it's kickoff time and both teams are obviously over-keyed for this one; much of the first quarter is sloppy and with three and a half minutes to go there is no score. Then, lightning strikes, literally. With 3:13 to go in the first quarter the game is halted because of thunderstorms roaring through Seattle and right over Century Link Field (The Clink). Football is played in nearly all kinds of weather and delays are rare. On this Sunday this game is the second one halted because of nearby lightning.

The game is delayed for exactly one hour and now I am worried – not so much about how the delay will affect my team (they had possession when play halted) but about whether or not I will be able to watch the entire game.

Shooters closes at 9PM local time and kickoff was at 6:30, more than enough time for the whole game. Even if it ran past nine, I know the staff has to clean up and I am certain I'll be able to stay. The one-hour delay changes everything; this game will run way past closing time. I am concerned.

I ask my waitress how long it takes to clean up after the doors are locked. She answers, "Don't worry, we don't leave until the last customer leaves."

"Well, uh," I stumble, "this game will probably end after 11 o'clock."

"That's ok," she bubbles.

Well, it's not okay. I don't want to be the only customer in the house, keeping an entire staff here two hours or more after closing time. So, I call the manager over and say, "I don't want to keep your people here longer than they have to be. Please let me know when they are done closing up and I will leave."

"Fine," he assures me.

The next thing I know, it's after 11, the game is over and the entire restaurant staff is sitting around the bar having a grand old time. I was amazed and impressed; THAT's customer service.

Chapter 17 – Sheridan, WY: The Trouble Down Below

Monday September 16 – Rapid City South Dakota-Sheridan, Wyoming

Wow, I can't believe I am heading for Sheridan, WY, my last "official" destination. I wrote from Rawlins, WY very early in my journey but I will break with my "rule" of not repeating in states for a couple of reasons.

Frankly, when I hit Rawlins in July, I wasn't at the top of my game. I'd just escaped my horrible adventure in Yellowstone National Park and had driven a long way. I stayed only one night and interviewed a small number of people. Their stories were valid and I wrote a short piece. So, Wyoming gets a second, and deeper look – a good thing, as it turns out.

In a way, it is unfortunate that Sheridan will mark the end of my search for The New America. In a perfect world, I would've headed south, then west from New York City for a longer drive home through vastly different cultures and economies.

Ben Stiller's 1994 flick "Reality Bites" comes to mind, though, because the title speaks volumes. In this case my reality that bites is financial. I simply cannot extend the trip south without leaning further on my family and friends whom have already contributed greatly to this project. Secondly, I am finally road weary and that's saying a lot. To say I love being on the road is putting it mildly. If I were a gangster, I'd be the wheelman. But, by the time I get home I will have driven over 10,000 miles in 70 days. Holy Crap! The Interstates are starting to look better and better.

Speaking of Interstates, my drive west to Sheridan will be mostly on I-90. Thankfully, as I head into Wyoming, Montana and the Idaho Panhandle into Washington, the freeway drive becomes more scenically palatable, starting with The Black Hills that extend from western South Dakota into eastern Wyoming.

The name Black Hills is a translation from the Lakota Pahá Sápa. The Hills *do* look black from afar because they are so dense with Evergreen Trees. I am surprised to learn they are the tallest mountains east of The Rockies, topping out with Harney Peak at 7,244 feet. This is deceiving because I am driving at an elevation of 3,200 feet so The Black Hills do look more like rolling hills than mountains. Whatever you call them, they exhibit an almost eerie, singular beauty.

Crossing the state line into Wyoming The Black Hills begin to spread out with more open prairie and ranches between them. Eventually The Black Hills fade into wide-open space and only the occasional cattle ranch mars the empty landscape. Even though I am more than 150 miles away, the Front Range of The Rocky Mountains appears from a ghostly fog on the horizon. About 50 miles further I am on a long straightaway and The Rockies rise up like a great wall. I-90 in the distance seems to disappear into the wall. I love optical illusions as they play with the eyes and your brain.

After 252 miles on I-90 I enter Sheridan, WY (est. pop. 17,598 in 2012) in the Tongue River Valley between The Black Hills and The Rockies. Whoo Hoo! The first freeway services sign shows a Starbucks logo. All I need is a good cigar store. Sheridan may claim only three exits but it is big enough for me. Have I said this about other towns as well? Probably. I am a simple man and sometimes so predictable.

Tuesday September 17 – Sheridan, WY

A Title Sheridan Wears Proudly

This city is named for General Philip Sheridan, a Union Cavalry leader during the Civil War. In 2006 *True West Magazine* named Sheridan as "The Top Western Town in America," something the city still touts; tourism is a big part of the economy. The other big draw is William Frederick "Buffalo Bill" Cody.

Bill Cody wasn't born in Sheridan; that would be Le Claire, Iowa Territory in 1846. Nor did he die here; that would be Denver, CO in 1917 – liver failure. What Cody did do here was own and operate the now-historic Sheridan Inn.

While in Sheridan I picked up a little known historical note on Buffalo Bill.

While Cody's legend is based on his (some say destructive) buffalo hunting skills and basically romanticizing the Wild West for the world, he apparently did some heroic work as an army scout in the Indian Wars.

He was a civilian scout mostly for the Third Cavalry Regiment from 1868-72. There are many varying and mostly vague accounts of how he earned the honor. My favorite version is also the most detailed. It comes from blogger Bill Hanks at Yahoo.com and goes like this:

"On July 11, 1869, Cody killed Chief Tall Bull and rescued a captured White woman. The skirmish was between the 5th Army and the Cheyenne Dog Soldiers. Tall bull was the leader of the Cheyenne. The Army was outnumbered 450 to 244 on that day. At the time, he was a civilian scout, working for the Army. He was a member of the Pawnee Scouts. On February 5th, 1917, 24 days after Cody's' death, the medal was declared invalid because he was a civilian and therefor wasn't eligible for the award. However the medal was restored to Cody, and eight other civilians, in 1989."

Sheridan was actually plotted in the early 1880s but it began to really flourish in 1892 when the Burlington Missouri Railroad extended to Sheridan. Shortly thereafter, the railroad commissioned construction of The Sheridan Inn to ensure travelers would have a decent room and a good place to eat.

The Sheridan Inn Today

By 1894 Bill Cody, by killing several thousand buffalo to feed railroad workers and the U.S. Army (for which he was a scout), had earned the "Buffalo Bill" sobriquet. He was also a consummate businessman and showman. His Wild West Show was already famous worldwide. In that year, Cody invested in The Sheridan Inn and for years used the property to audition acts for his show.

Sadly, the Inn has a ragged history with many owners since Cody's day. Now, it is closed and a dilapidated shell of itself. There is talk of new owners. I hope so; it can once again be a grand structure and serious tourist attraction for Sheridan. The town needs it.

While ranching and tourism are important here, when I was in Rawlins I heard that the state of Wyoming receives most of its revenue from the energy production industry and, as a result, avoided a big hit from the recession. In Sheridan I confirm the first fact and learn the second is only partially true.

Unemployment in Sheridan has dropped from a high of almost eight percent in 2010 to the low fives now. In 2012 home sales rebounded from a low of 48 in 2011 to 71 in 2012. But there are problems still and they bubble – literally – just below the surface.

Twenty-nine year old Ryan is a coal miner. He is walking down Main Street with his wife and baby daughter. He tells me the mine in which he works produces a different kind of coal than that of the other mines. His company's coal is shipped by rail to The Port of Vancouver, British Columbia where it is shipped to Asia and so the recession passed him by. The others, he says, weren't so lucky.

"Prices and production dropped in the other mines around the state," he tells me. "The mine next to us laid off half their work force during the slowdown, hundreds of people lost their jobs."

Fifty-five year old Don Barrett works above ground but his living is down below. He is an accountant for one of the local natural gas exploration companies.

"Business was good until natural gas prices collapsed during the recession and they still haven't come back. It's a big problem. About two-thirds of our employees were laid off, about 70 people. Even the oil industry suffered."

In 2011 economists predicted Wyoming's energy-based revenue would "flatten." By last year, as prices continued to drop, Governor Matt Mead ordered an additional eight percent in budget cuts for fiscal 2013.

Chapter 18 – Found, The New America

Tuesday September 17-Thursday September 19 – Sheridan, WY-Butte, MT-Spokane, WA-Renton, WA

After completing my final interviews in Sheridan and writing them up, I make a beeline for home and hearth. Even so, it is still a three-day drive. Now that my work is done I can revisit a couple of favorite campgrounds from early in the journey – the Beaverhead-Deerlodge National Forest near Butte, MT (where a galloping herd of elk greeted me at sunrise one day) and Riverside State Park near Spokane, WA, out in the boonies but ten minutes from downtown.

I relax and enjoy driving I-90 as it heads for the Rocky Mountains. From this point on, even the Interstate cannot detract from some of the most beautiful country in America.

Seventy days and 10,244 miles, I am home. In a sense, it feels strange to be off the road. Faithful canine companion Trooper and I have been in a pleasant routine. Every couple of days it's been a new location, new people, new experiences and new stories. All of a sudden, it's over and I am at loose ends. Trooper is nonplussed.

As road weary as I am, it's been an amazing journey and I know I will soon miss being on the road. It may be a cliché but it has truly been the trip of a lifetime. And, as good as it is to be home, I feel a bit of a letdown.

The good news is, I found The New America. The better news is a lot of the best characteristics of the "Old America" remain intact – perseverance, personal strength, a healthy patriotism and, most of all, resilience. The bad news is, there is no widespread national recovery yet.

In many of the places I visited, the recession arrived late and, in some places, hasn't left. There is still a lot of pain and suffering in America. I don't know if this is a story the denizens of Washington, D.C. want to hide or if they are simply unaware of what's going on outside The Beltway.

While it's hard to generalize, I saw enough similarities and trends to make some overall observations, with a caveat. I visited "only" 16 states and 26 communities, far short of my initial goals.

My original plan was to hit as many different regions as possible but return west in time to avoid an autumnal bad weather re-crossing of the Rocky Mountains. I wanted to stay out of the big cities and visit what I call the real America. Eastbound I was going to work my way down from the Pacific Northwest toward the Denver-area, across America's mid-section, finally curving up to New York City. That part of the plan worked out fine.

My hope for the return trip was to travel through Dixie and the Southwest to capture their widely differing economies and cultures. In that way, I hoped to experience a full cross-section of America's recessionary experience. It was not to be. Gas prices and my below poverty-level income – read that living on Social Security – conspired to restrict my journey. Instead of turning south from New York, I had no choice but to take a more direct route home across the top of America. Still, there was much to observe and learn.

Uncle Fed tells us America's economy is growing at the rate of two-and-a-half-percent a year. All the charts and forecasts may point that way but don't tell it to people in towns like Dodge City and Fredonia, KS. In Dodge City, where tourism and farming drive the economy, the recession didn't show up until recently. Tourism has dropped by a third. The cattle business – once Dodge City's claim to fame – is all but dying. The small, isolated town of Fredonia is literally dying.

Don't mention it either to the retailers in downtown Cooperstown, NY, home of Major League Baseball's Hall of Fame and where tourism is king. Most of them sell baseball related merchandise and as The Hall goes so goes their business. It's all down anywhere from 10-25 percent, both visitors and business.

Many small towns and cities depend on one or two big manufacturers for their economic health. In town after town I heard stories of factories closing and tossing hundreds of people out of work. Or, in the case of Sheridan, WY, it was the mines. Energy production might be Wyoming's largest industry now and around Sheridan it is coal, natural gas and oil. During the recession the coal prices dropped and some mines closed while others cut back drastically on production.

Fifty-five year old Don Barrett is an accountant who works in the natural gas industry. He told me, "Business was good until natural gas prices collapsed during the recession and they still haven't come back. It's a big problem. About two-thirds of our employees were laid off, about 70 people. Even the oil industry suffered."

In many of these small towns and cities the ripple affects are still rippling; businesses are closing, the housing market is still slow and unemployment remains high. Small city downtowns across America are pockmarked with empty stores for rent or sale. Their decline began with the advent of Wal-Mart and other big box stores but the recession exacerbated their demise. In tiny Delphi, Indiana, I interviewed a third generation appliance storeowner in front of his shop on the town's courthouse square. "There used to be 40 viable businesses in the square," he told me. "We had traffic control and you couldn't find parking. The recession accelerated the process. Today I'll bet there aren't five viable businesses here."

Keokuk, Iowa is still home to a very large employer– French multi-national food products manufacturer Roquette – but the recession still left its mark. Other, smaller manufacturers closed and unemployment still hovers at around 10 percent.

These are just a few examples of the many small towns and cities I visited that are still in the grip of economic hardship.

Conversely, there are pockets of America where the recession had little or no major affect; places like Butte, Montana and Rapid City, South Dakota. In the former, an economy diversified away from the area's historic roots in mining made the difference. In the latter, a proactive and dogged private sector downtown development group refused to let a slump in the energy production business drag the city into a slide. The result is a vibrant downtown Rapid City.

La Crosse, Wisconsin is another small city that dodged the economic bullet. The combination of strong national companies based there and a large health care presence, led by the Mayo Clinic, protected this city of 51,647 (in 2012). The historic and well preserved downtown is diverse and healthy. I drove around and saw no closed, empty shops.

When I set out on my journey I suspected The Great Recession had changed

America forever. I wasn't surprised to have my suspicion confirmed. What did surprise me was how deeply the downturn reached into the American psyche.

The two prime examples:

- The male ego – it's no secret that in many homes today, both spouses have careers. The surprise here was how many men took a blow to their testosterone when they lost their jobs while their wives kept theirs. "I've always seen myself as being able to provide for my family," they told me. "It's been a huge blow to my self-esteem that I am not the one putting the bread on the table."

- Parenting – "The recession made me change the way I parent my children," was a surprisingly common theme. "It used to be that I gave my kids whatever they needed or wanted. Now, they have to know how hard it is to pay for those things."

Some other recurring themes:

- "We were forced to cut spending on a lot of things we didn't really need. We don't go out to the movies or for dinner as much as we used to."

- "I've become much more conservative in how I manage my personal finances. Even when this thing is over, I will never go back to the old way of just spending money because I can."

- "I was forced to dip into my savings or retirement (in many cases to the tune of five figures). As a result, I'm making sure I save more."

- "We are taking vacations closer to home."
    - From the couple in the equestrian campground near Spokane, Wa, "We used to go wherever we wanted. Now, we have to save for a month to come here, just 15 minutes from home."
    - To the family from Chicago, "We really couldn't afford a distant vacation this year, so we just drove to Springfield (IL)."

- "I had to turn to my family for help." And, it wasn't only kids going back to Mom & Dad; I talked to fathers living with their kids and Aunts/Uncles living with nieces or nephews.

- "The whole experience made me stronger and tougher."

- "I'm much more skeptical about what I hear and whom I trust." Sadly, I heard this more and more from young people.

- "Looks like I'll be working a few more years before I can retire." Whether they had to dip into their retirement funds or their funds took a dive, many Americans' later years look a lot different now.

- American Flags – A major trend and not a surprising one – yes, there is the widespread mistrust and disgust with the aforementioned denizens of D.C. Yet, we still love America. I saw American Flags displayed everywhere; on downtown streets, flying from front porches, from business storefronts and in store windows. I saw American Flag decals on countless pickup trucks, RVs and family sedans. Even in a town that is wallowing in poverty and dying, I saw in a city park the biggest American Flag I've ever seen proudly waving in a stiff breeze.

- The Wind in the Willows – Like a soft summer breeze, the wind energy production industry has quietly established itself in America. Regardless of geography, huge wind farms are everywhere.

I don't know if you can call the next item a trend, per se but I must write about this American subculture. I preferred to find campsites in publicly owned properties, national parks or forests, Army Corps of Engineers' sites, state, county or city parks. When there were no public facilities near a place I wanted to visit, I resorted to private campgrounds, RV or trailer parks.

Normally, I hate to characterize entire groups of people with broad generalizations but there is a subgroup of American society that easily fits a general description and it's not a pretty one. Some call them po' White trash while others use the term trailer trash. Whatever you call 'em, they're out there and they are generally poor and under-educated. Their trailers are on rented property; they might also farm on rented land. Others live in "trailer parks" dedicated only to fulltime residents while still others set up permanent or quasi-permanent residency in RV/trailer parks. I camped in several of the latter.

Most of these folks are nice, neighborly and, given the chance, hard-working Americans. There are some, however, who are angry at their circumstances and their anger is manifested in any number of ways, none of them productive. Often it is simply grumpiness but sometimes it more severe. The worst example I witnessed was the child abusing couple trailering behind me in Ft. Loramie State Park, OH. The image will always be with me of this bleached blonde heavy-set woman in a floating muu muu yelling, bullying, spanking and then slapping a terrified four-year old girl. The girl's only crime was crying.

The Highs and the Lows

Best Ride
2006 Jeep Liberty – Before hitting the road my Jeep had 60,000 miles on it. It was running fine but I still spent $400 on a full going over, oil change, sparkplugs, new wipers and all other fluids. For 10,244 miles the Jeep took a lickin' and kept on tickin'.

Worst Day
No contest, 20-hours in Yellowstone National Park – thievery, attempted burglary, traffic jams, car crashes and a camping ghetto akin to one of those huge, crowded apartment complexes across the Hudson River from upper Manhattan. I couldn't get out of there fast enough.

Best Day
Escaping Missouri's biblical rains would've been enough. I was out of money and spent seven soaked days mostly watching the rain from the rear cargo area of the Jeep. Finally making my escape, I had to drive all the way to Central Illinois to get away from the storms.

What took the day from good to GREAT was my stopover in St. Louis. Not only did I find a premium cigar store on The Hill (the city's famous and brazenly Italian neighborhood), the proprietor steered me to Gioia's Deli (1934 Macklind Ave. 314-776-9410) that served up without a doubt the best Italian hero sandwich I've ever eaten. Don't even look at the menu, just order the hot Italian salami sandwich and ask the person behind the counter to help you with the add-ons.

What took the day from great to SPECTACULAR was my visit to Yogi Berra's boyhood home and the interview with his grand-niece, who happened to be sitting on the porch.

Best Coffee House That Isn't a Starbucks
The Stagecoach in Cooperstown, NY (31 Pioneer St. 607-542-6229) is a

family owned and operated café that serves up great espresso drinks, excellent food and a heaping handful of friendly service. The free Wi-Fi is a bonus and made the place my base of operations in Cooperstown.

Worst Day on the Road – Pop-Top Cargo Box

I was flying down the interstate at my usual seven miles over the speed limit when a car pulls up along side me and the passenger starts pointing to the roof of the Jeep. I know my cargo box is funky because of the attempted break-in at Yellowstone. Instead of easily prying open the two cheap locks on the side of the box, the idiots tried to force their way in by breaking the back hinge. As a result, the box's lid does not align correctly and the locks are even less secure than before. So I know something is not right upstairs.

I pull to the shoulder, engage the emergency flasher and hop out to take a look. Sure enough, both locks have disengaged. Luckily, there are clamps at either end of the box to keep the lid down in just such a situation so I'm wondering what the mobile Good Samaritan saw. I take another look and notice the rear clamp is also disengaged. That's not good.

I climb to the Jeep's roof and open the box. Both my sleeping bag and pillow are gone, disappeared, poof. I can live without the pillow but it will cost at least $40 I can't afford to replace the sleeping bag.

Best Bang For the Buck

Several years ago I spent $39.95 on a tiny Sony digital voice recorder. It's no bigger than one of those old five stick gum packs (remember those?). I carried it in my pants pocket throughout the trip. Not only did I record my interviews but also any thoughts, observations, etc. It allowed me to accurately and more completely blog as I went.

Best Camping at State Parks

Based on their bathrooms alone, I have to go with New York and Pennsylvania. Showers are at a premium on the road and, for the most part they are grimy, moldy and often smelly. Flip-flops on your feet are an anti-fungal requirement. You are often accompanied by hundreds of dead insects. Not so in these two states, their rest rooms are spotless.

Most Embarrassing Moment

Can you embarrass yourself when there's no one around? I did.

First campground shower early in my trip – I forgot to bring my towel. No problem, right? There are always paper towels. Wrong. I guess to save money most publicly owned campgrounds have dispensed with paper towel dispensers and rely on electric dryers. Have you ever tried to dry your entire body with a wall mounted electric dryer? It ain't pretty and adds a whole new dimension to the term blowjob.

Best Meals I Didn't Grill or Pay For
Where else? New York City, more specifically, Brooklyn's Park Slope. Big brother Steve takes very seriously his role as titular head of the family and, he worries about me out on the road all by myself. When I got to the "auld sod" for a visit, he absolutely spoils me with freshly made New York bagels, dinner at the neighborhood Italian joint and lunch at the local Chinese place. Aaaaaaah.

Scariest Moment – Apprehended in the Missouri Ozarks
It was more like a second but you can't help but gasp when you think you're pulling over for a routine traffic stop and two other Sheriff's cruisers screech in right after the first one with their blue lights flashing. Of course, the fear immediately subsided; there was no plausible reason for all the law enforcement attention. It seems they had me confused with an escaped convict. I drove away from the encounter with a secret smile on my face; they gave me something about which to write.

Moment Where I Almost Lost It
Off Runway 24B at the former Floyd Bennett Naval Air Base in Brooklyn I encountered dear kindly National Parks Police Officer Asshole. Contrary to popular myth, most New Yorkers are very nice, especially to out-of-towners. They are rushed and brusque, but very nice and helpful. Not so for Officer Asshole. He was just plain nasty.

The air base is now a National Recreation Area and home to one of the two publicly owned campgrounds in the city. Whatever you call it, it is still an air base and poorly signed at that. There is no signage directing you to a registration place or to the campsites.

After getting directions to the sign-in place and receiving a poorly printed map of the "campground," I wandered aimlessly for 30-minutes unable to locate my tent site. Finally, pulling out of a narrow dead-end dirt lane, Officer A**hole appears about 20-30 yards in front of the Jeep with his hand up. I slowed to a crawl and inched nearer to him, which obviously blew his very short fuse because the ensuing conversation, dominated by the officer, took place mostly in **bold letters**.

It started off with, "**Didn't you understand my command to STOP?**" And went downhill from there. He was pissed because I'd entered a "road" labeled – but hidden behind bushes – with a battered "Do Not Enter" sign.

Even after I explained that I was lost, and had been for a half hour, Officer Asshole continued to berate and harass me, complete with a **boldly** stated lecture on the vehicle traffic code. When I opened the glove box for my registration he noticed a baggie and **ordered** me out of the car to explain its contents. It contained the one remaining pill that protected Trooper from heartworm.

Nonetheless, he tried looking through the darkly tinted rear windows with visions of a drug bust dancing in his head and I could smell the wood burning; he was contemplating a complete search. Have you ever seen the inside of a vehicle that's been on a road trip for more than 6,000 miles? It's a friggin' cramped and crowded mess.

Barely holding on to my withered patience I seized the moment. Opening the tailgate I calmly offered, "Go ahead, have a look."

He stuck his head inside for a quick glance and deferred. Asshole.

Best Downtown – Rapid City, SD

I can't explain why but I wasn't really looking forward to Rapid City. Maybe it's the name, if not boring, it sounds fictitious. I learn quickly; Rapid City is anything but boring. It's downtown is lively and diverse with outdoor cafes, souvenir shops, galleries and regular retail stores. There is public art on nearly every downtown corner and the vibe is positive, almost electric.

Most Heart rending Interview

I was wrapping up my interviews in Fredonia, Kansas, a small off-the-beaten-path town that is wallowing and dying in the arms of the recession. She was a preacher ministering to the town's children and their families.

"I've seen a decline for several years but last year it accelerated and I can tell this year will be worse," she told me.

"We send out our vans to pick up and feed kids every day, not just church kids. We can see that family life is changing. It's not uncommon for the kids to have one or both parents in jail; thievery is on the upswing. I see more abuse and neglect with the children, a lack of discipline."

"The schools are stepping in and feeding families, as are the churches. The number of families we feed each week has almost doubled. And, families are leaving town. Over the last few years we've lost 25% of our congregation."

"I'm just waiting on the Lord," she says. "God works miracles. I'm ready to see Him provide and I pray all the time. More and more, though, when I pray I am also crying."

Most Awe-Inspiring Moment
Mt. Rushmore! The mountain is much smaller than I imagined but it doesn't matter. Pictures don't do it justice. The carvings are electric and magnificent. After photographing it from every angle, I get back in the Jeep and sit there for I don't know how long, just staring at Mt. Rushmore.

Best Thing About the Whole Trip
Doing it!

Lee Somerstein

Chapter 19 – Afterward: Welcome to Baristaville

October 16 - Renton, WA

Sometimes the solution to a problem is right in front of you and you still can't find it. Thus was it for me.

If you followed my recent summer journey across America, you know of my loyalty to Starbucks. Not only did Howard Schultz's empire serve as my office nationwide – with its free WiFi and stay-as-long-as-you-want policy – I just love the coffee. I've been a customer since 1974. That's B.H., Before Howard.

While I was on the road I did a lot of thinking; that's one of the major bennies of a road trip, enjoying the time with yourself and using it productively. I decided I needed to do something to drag myself above the poverty line, something not related to either writing or my other career skills.

This was cathartic; I realized that I'd let my ego keep me down. Ever since my position at Safeco Insurance disappeared in January 2008 I'd devoted my job search and then my entrepreneurial experiment(s) to the things that always brought the bacon home: media, public relations and marketing. Why not? These were all areas in which I had long experience, success and considerable skills. Yet, the bacon eluded me. I kept running into the term "over qualified" which is the legal way of saying "too old."

With my ego blocking the way, I never considered taking a lesser position outside of my now defunct career track to augment my barely survivable social security benefit. Somewhere between Fredonia, NY and Grand Rapids, SD my ego fell by the roadside. I knew when I returned home I would look for a lower wage job to make things financially better. And, I knew I would only apply with one company, Starbucks.

So, here I am, a little more than one month after my return, sitting in *my* Starbucks store writing this piece. I've just completed my first two days of barista training and it feels like I've been here forever. That's not to say it's easy. Au contraire, my friend; even though it is a minimum wage (plus tips) position, there is a mountain of information to absorb and a potential for great stress to absorb.

Frankly, I was a bit intimidated about learning the drinks. Starbucks is committed to making the perfect drink for everyone, no matter how the customer might add, twist, subtract or blow up the original recipe. In two training days this baby barista was bombarded with:

- The Starbucks culture and history
- How to be a good partner (partner not employee)
- How to get a food service worker's card
- How to maintain store cleanliness and operation
- Number of shots per cup size
- Number of syrup pumps per drink and cup size
- Number of flavor and/or protein scoops per drink and cup size
- How to make a variety of blended drinks
- How to correctly brew just plain coffee
- How to make that special Starbucks hot chocolate
- How to make a variety of tea drinks
- How to operate the complex screen on the cash till
    - while taking orders
    - and writing the correct codes on the cup
    - after you learn all the correct codes
- And various other duties as assigned.

It is both daunting and challenging yet, by the end of my first day I was providing store support, a rotation of duties that includes keeping the fresh brewed coffee fresh brewed, replenishing supplies, cups, lids, sleeves et al, cleaning the lobby and the bathrooms and other duties as assigned.

On my second day I began practicing drink prep on a spare machine and, ultimately, taking orders at one of the tills. Thankfully, my excellent trainer was always beside me with both correction and encouragement. I was surprised to learn that making the drinks was easier than thinking about making the drinks. Other baristas I've queried told me it took them two-to-three months to master the basic recipes, a bit longer for the grande half-caf soy 180 degree 13 pump peppermint mocha with extra whipped cream drinks and their ilk.

I also met my first in-store anti-Semite, a regular patron at this location, who put my customer service skills to the extreme test. I think it was his comment that, "The Jews run all the news and entertainment media," that tipped me off. My restraint was admirable to say the least.

All in all, though, the hours have flown by, my fellow partners – 30-to-40 years my junior – are welcoming and helpful and I feel at home in Baristaville.

ABOUT THE AUTHOR

Lee Somerstein has been blogging under the Nom de Plume LeeZard since 1997. He has a lot to say, as the header explains at LEEZARD ON LIFE: "LeeZard observes life and writes commentary, opinion and humor about politics, people, news events - heck, anything that strikes his fancy."

Mr. Somerstein began his professional writing career as a broadcast journalist, network correspondent and editor. Over the course of his 20 years as a broadcaster, he won numerous local and national awards.

As a freelance writer based in Seattle, Mr. Somerstein has published in New York Newsday, The Seattle Times, The Seattle Post-Intelligencer and The Seattle Weekly, to name a few.

The truth is, Lee Somerstein really began writing when he was 10-years old. It was Grandpa Joe's fault; when the young LeeZard was in the fourth grade, Grandpa started challenging him to write stories.

But, why does Lee Somerstein write? His answer:
"It certainly isn't for the money (although that would be nice). Every writer, once they find their 'voice,' seeks out his audience. But, you need more than a voice for that audience to find you, stay with you and pass you around like a cheap date; you have to have things to say. I have things to say and I tell a damned good story.

For one thing, I've led a more interesting life than most: good, bad, awful, exciting, scary, sometimes inspired (maybe even inspiring) and sometimes downright stupid. That's not bragging or arrogance, it's just a fact.

If I make someone laugh, cry, angry or think, I'll consider myself a successful writer.

Most importantly, however, I've overcome tremendous obstacles to not only write but to stay alive. If the lessons I've learned in life and my will to survive inspire one person; If someone is at their absolute bottom and says, 'If that guy can make it so can I," I will consider myself a very successful writer."

www.ingramcontent.com/pod-product-compliance
Lightning Source LLC
Chambersburg PA
CBHW051807170526
45167CB00005B/1911